U'REN: A LOOK BACK

William Simon U'Ren, age 72.

This portrait was taken in 1931 by Henry Berger Jr. (1877–1939) at Berger's studio in Portland, Oregon. negative # 12783.

U'REN
A LOOK BACK

A REVEALING COLLECTION OF HISTORIC
MAGAZINE ARTICLES, NEWSPAPER STORIES,
EDITORIALS, ADVERTISEMENTS, ESSAYS, AND
OTHER INTERESTING FACTS, PRESENTED FOR
THE EDIFICATION OF STUDENTS OF ALL AGES,
AS WELL AS ALL CITIZENS OF GOOD WILL
SEEKING GOOD GOVERNMENT, AND SHOWING
HOW ONE WILLIAM S. U'REN FOUGHT TO
BRING DIRECT DEMOCRACY TO OREGON

EDITED WITH COMMENTARY BY
John F. Williams, Jr.

RESEARCHED WITH COMMENTARY BY
J. F. Williams

U'Ren: A Look Back   ISBN: 978-1-7357623-0-2

Published By

MARCH OF THE MIND, LLC
Thinking Is Everyone's Business

marchofthemind.com

marchofthemind@gmail.com

MANUFACTURED IN THE UNITED STATES OF AMERICA

FIRST PRINTING: JANUARY 2021

10 9 8 7 6 5 4 3 2   25 24 23 22 21

VERSION 2021.1

THIS WORK IS DEDICATED TO THE MEMORY OF

OREGON CITY MAYOR
EDWARD ALLICK
5 MARCH 1934–29 MARCH 2019

AND

OREGON CITY MAYOR
DONALD G. ANDERSEN
5 APRIL 1932–7 JULY 2017

These two Oregon City leaders gave countless hours of their time to their fellow citizens through their selfless volunteer government service. Both understood the concept of direct democracy as established in Oregon through the labors of William S. U'Ren.

They generously shared their wisdom, knowledge, and friendship with the editor.

CONTENTS

The William S. U'Ren memorial plaque at the Clackamas
County Courthouse in downtown Oregon City.

LOCATION: 807 MAIN STREET, OREGON CITY, OREGON (45.358611, -122.607222)

PHOTO CREDIT: JOHN F. WILLIAMS, JR.

PREFACE

M Y INTEREST IN OREGON HISTORY comes from the fact that my great-grandfather, William Blodgett, and his wife Aseneth, arrived in Oregon in 1847 via the southern route—the Applegate Trail—and established a 620-acre land claim west of Corvallis near present-day Blodgett, Oregon.

My interest in William Simon U'Ren (accent the last syllable), who came to Oregon 42-years later, began soon after my 1992 retirement to historic Oregon City, Oregon. One day, while walking past the Clackamas County Courthouse, I spotted a memorial plaque—see the previous page—honoring U'Ren.

IN HONOR OF

WILLIAM SIMON U'REN

BLACKSMITH • LAWYER • POLITICAL REFORMER

Author of Oregon's constitutional provisions for the **Initiative, Referendum & Recall** giving the people control of law making and lawmakers and known in his lifetime as father of Oregon's enlightened system of government. This memorial is dedicated in gratitude by the Oregon City Hilltop boosters and by friends and admirers on behalf of the people of Oregon.

APRIL, 1977

I didn't know about U'Ren and what he'd accomplished. Although I had been educated in the public schools of nearby Portland, and was actively interested in politics, I drew a blank reading the plaque's inscription. I wanted to learn more about the man the memorial praised.

I did just that using the standard references. Then in 2019, hoping to make U'Ren known to more people, I decided to republish a profile of U'Ren written by Lincoln Steffens in 1908, along with other interesting material about U'Ren in the public domain.

I enlisted my son to be my researcher and publisher, and off we went, spending the next year happily learning about William S. U'Ren, his family, the people around him, and the events of his time not usually found in the standard articles and references about him. Our investigation was made possible by the World Wide Web and the ongoing digitalization of many historical records previously available only in books and microfilm at distant libraries.

This work is not a formal biography of U'Ren. It's a collection of newspapers stories, magazine articles, book excerpts, and more, most entertaining, sharp, sometimes humorous, all well-written, about U'Ren and the events of his lifetime. Your humble editors have added commentary and footnotes after consulting reference materials found on the World Wide Web, such as historical studies, census reports, directories, probate records, passport filings, etc., in an attempted to do what a historian might do—make inferences, comment on patterns, and make judgments on past events.

U'Ren went from humble beginnings in Wisconsin to being an important and influential historical figure in Oregon and the United States, loved by many, but also feared and despised by others. You will be surprised about some of the things you'll read here. And you'll be reminded that some things in this world never change.

John F. Williams, Jr.
Oregon City, Oregon

ABOUT THIS BOOK

THIS BOOK IS A COLLECTION of works published between 1868 and 1925 about William S. U'Ren. A modern reader may find some of the constructions, phrases, colloquialisms, and word spellings in the writings unfamiliar or outdated.

To minimize confusion over common first names and different spellings of the Uren surname, family members are referred to as follows:

THE UREN FAMILY

WILLIAM SIMON (1859–1949) —» WILLIAM U'REN, W. S. U'REN

WILLIAM RICHARD (1834–1927) (*father*) —» W. R. UREN

FRANCES JANE (1837–1928) (*mother*) —» FRANCES UREN

SELENA ANN (1861–1936) (*sister*) —» SELENA UREN

THOMAS ANDREW (1863–1900) (*brother*) —» T. A. UREN

CHARLES PHILIP (1868–1950) (*brother*) —» C. P. UREN

FRANCES MARY (1873–1968) (*sister*) —» FRANCES M. UREN

Abbreviations and signs used:

c. —» circa (i.e., approximately).

§ § § —» This sign in the text indicates that content not germane to the topic has been removed.

U'REN: A LOOK BACK

CHRONOLOGY

The Life of William Simon U'Ren

DATE (AGE)	EVENT
1859 (0)	Born 10 JANUARY at Lancaster, Wisconsin to William Richard (25) and Frances Jane (Ivey) (21) Uren.
	Oregon admitted to the Union on 14 FEBRUARY.
1861 (2)	Uren family lived in Calumet, Michigan from 1861 to at least 1863.
1866 (7)	Uren family lived in the Territory of Colorado in 1866 and 1867.
1868 (9)	Uren family lived in Cheyenne, Territory of Wyoming.
1870 (11)	Uren family lived in Nebraska from 1870 to 1877, leaving at the end of that year for Colorado.
1878 (19)	William worked as a laborer at a mine, then as a blacksmith's helper in Denver; during winter, attended evening classes at a business college.
1880 (21)	Read law at the firm of France & Rogers in Denver; joined the Republican Party.

DATE (AGE)	EVENT
1881 (22)	Admitted to Colorado Bar on 31 JANUARY.
	Practiced law in Aspen, Colorado and was Pritkin County's first County Attorney.
	Moved to Tin Cup, Colorado. Practiced law and published *The Garfield Banner* for a time.
	The Uren family, except for William, moved to The Dalles, Oregon.
1882 (23)	Practiced law in Tin Cup until the summer of 1887.
1887 (28)	Left for California.
1888 (29)	Lived in the Hawaiian Islands.
1889 (30)	Stayed at family's sheep ranch in Bake Oven, Oregon.
1890 (31)	Settled in Oregon.
	Met Edward W. Bingham; worked on the campaign for the Australian Ballot System.
1891 (32)	Lived in Portland at a boarding house in what was then called 'South Portland' and worked as a laborer.
	Met Seth Lewelling in Milwaukie, Oregon.

DATE (AGE)	EVENT
1892 (33)	Joined Seth Lewelling's nursery business and lived in a cabin on the Lewelling's property.
	Learned about Switzerland's use of the Initiative and Referendum.
1893 (34)	Led new movement for the Initiative and Referendum in Oregon as Secretary of the Direct Legislation League Committee.
1896 (37)	Elected as a Representative to the 1897 Oregon Legislature for the Populist Party.
1897 (38)	Was a key leader in the Oregon Legislature's infamous 'hold-up' session.
	Non-Partisan Direct Legislation League, W. S. U'Ren secretary, replaced the Direct Legislation League Committee.
1898 (39)	Returned to the practice of law with an office in Oregon City, Oregon.
	Ran for Oregon State Senate but lost.
	Elected to the Executive Committee of the National Direct Legislation League.
1900 (41)	Lived in Gladstone, Oregon at his parent's house.
	Traveled to South Africa in JULY, after the death there, of his brother T. A. U'Ren.

DATE (AGE)	EVENT
1901 (42)	Formed law partnership with Christian Schuebel in Oregon City, Oregon. Married Mary Beharrell.
1902 (43)	Constitutional amendment adding Initiative and Referendum powers approved by Oregon voters.
1905 (46)	The People's Power League, W. S. U'Ren secretary, formed in DECEMBER.
1907 (48)	Lived with his wife in a three-room house on two river-front acres in the Greenpoint addition of Oregon City, Oregon. Interviewed by the famous journalist Lincoln Steffens.
1908 (49)	Sold his Greenpoint house and rented the residence of Judge Thomas F. Ryan's at 715 5th Street in upper Oregon City.
1909 (50)	Visited the Short Ballot Association's secretary, Richard S. Childs, in New York. Became Secretary of Oregon Single Tax League.
1911 (52)	In MAY, escorted Governor Woodrow Wilson from California into Oregon.

DATE (AGE)	EVENT
1914 (55)	Moved to Portland, Oregon.
	Ran for Governor of Oregon as an independent but lost.
	Moved law office to Portland in JULY and added Frank C. Hesse as a partner.
1915 (56)	Law partnership with Schuebel ends.
	U'Ren and Hesse moved their law office to the Oregonian Building.
1918 (59)	Lived at 524 SE 16th Avenue in Portland.
	Became a member of the American Civil Liberties Union's (ACLU) national board. Served on that board until 1935.
1924 (65)	Lived at 2145 NW Flanders Street in Portland.
1927 (68)	Lived at the Ambassador Apartments at 1209 SW 6th Avenue, number 802, in Portland.
1931 (72)	Lived at 2405 NE 16th Avenue in Portland.
1932 (73)	Ran for Oregon House of Representatives but lost. Ran again for same office in 1934 but lost again.
1934 (75)	Lived at the Ambassador Apartments at 1209 SW 6th Avenue, number 805, in Portland.

DATE (AGE)	EVENT
1949 (90)	William Simon U'Ren died from pneumonia on 8 MARCH in Portland, Oregon. Mary U'Ren died two months later [24].

I

INITIATIVE & REFERENDUM: 1893–1902

1

U'REN SHAPES OREGON'S 'BIG STICK'

W E START WITH AN EXCERPT from an article written by Lucius Curtis 'Lute' Pease (1869–1963) and found in the MAY 1907 issue of *The Pacific Monthly*.[1]

Pease was a reporter and cartoonist for *The Oregonian* from 1895 to 1897, and then again from 1902 to 1905.[2]

Pease joined *The Pacific Monthly* in 1905 as an author and artist; he became its editor in 1907.

He later moved to New Jersey and became a political cartoonist on the staff of the *Newark Evening News*. He worked there for the next forty years, winning a Pulitzer Prize for Editorial Cartooning in 1949.

Pease had seen U'Ren and his associates in action; he was one of the first writers to have grasped the far-reaching and revolutionary character of their project. What follows is an intelligent, straight-forward account of how Oregon came to adopt the Initiative and Referendum.

---

[1] *The Pacific Monthly* was published in Portland, Oregon from 1898 until 1911, when it was purchased by the Southern Pacific Railroad and merged with its magazine, *Sunset*—Ed.

[2] From 1897 to 1902, Pease hunted for gold and adventure in the Yukon and Alaska—Ed.

The Initiative and Referendum—Oregon's "Big Stick"

By Lute Pease

In the white heat of a municipal campaign in one of the largest cities of the Northwest not many years ago, I heard a certain prominent lawyer harangue a huge street gathering. In denouncing one of the Mayoralty candidates, he flung about like a Dervish, perspired like a harvest hand, roared and pawed like an excited bogey, and after scraping raw the language for expressions of disapproval, reached his climax in a sort of scream.

"And, fellow citizens, he—he believes in the 'nish'tive and referENdum!"

His audience stared, jaw-fallen. What meant the sinister phrase? Evidently nothing less than socialism, anarchy, horrors and disaster.

The candidate was defeated, but he is still one of the reform leaders of his state—Washington—and has helped to push forward the movement for direct legislation to the point of adoption of at least one of the important measures now being tested by Oregon—and, in a much weaker form, by a few other states. Oklahoma, however, has just adopted the Oregon law entire, and Dakota is considering similar action.

A democracy is defined by Noah Webster as a "form of government in which the supreme power is retained and directly exercised by the people." The fathers organized for us a republican form of government; that is the people are required by the National Constitution to delegate their powers to the representatives elected by them. But by the adoption of the constitutional amendment [shown in Appendix E], Oregon has become a pure democracy. A peaceful revolution has been accomplished, in this state at least—a revolution that bids fair to spread throughout the Union. The measure has stirred wide discussion; all sorts of beneficent or evil results have been prophesied for or against it. In its entirety, the Oregon measure is declared to be more radical than the form in vogue in the most radical cantons of Switzerland whence the idea was borrowed. Various writers have given it some attention, but comparatively few people other than its originators seem to have grasped more than a hint of its far-reaching and revolutionary character. When one considers that it emasculates the state legislature; that it opens the avenues for all manner of political innovations; and that intelligently used it eliminates the boss, the machine and the grafter, and makes absolute the will of a majority of the voters, one realizes that the people of Oregon wield a most formidable weapon.

It has been said that every form of government except a pure democracy has been weighed and found wanting. Oregon seems to be in a position to give a practical test to the latter form. As, a hundred years since, men argued that the republican method must be the ideal; today many contend that a purely democratic government, if not ideal, must certainly be an improvement. And of course none but the thoughtless would assert that anything man has made, man cannot with time and study improve upon. As Judge Stephen A. Lowell, of Oregon, said in a famous speech on direct legislation:

> Venerable and majestic as is a legislative system which has stood for a hundred years, neither age nor majesty is a guarantee that it ought not to give way to something better.

It was the theory of a majority of the framers of the Federal Constitution—"bundle of compromises" as it has been termed—that the people cannot be trusted to wisely exercise supreme power; that it is safer for them to delegate the law-making authority to a chosen few who would also be best qualified to choose the United States Senators, and to another yet more choice few who should select the President.

More than a century's test of this theory has demonstrated even to the most vociferous defender of "our sacred institutions" the presence of a number of defects. For many years have not the following charges vexed our dull ears?

"Our best people take little personal interest in politics because the issues are manufactured by designing politicians and the candidates are but their dummies.

"Having no law-making responsibility, the majority of voters are merely slaves to party, and are handled like sheep by unscrupulous politicians.

"Shrewd bosses, with cunningly organized machines, control the offices and secure laws safely to rob the people.

"State legislatures are deadlocked or held up by rival factions in Senatorial elections, interfering with all other functions of such bodies, at great cost to the people.

"Our representatives do not represent the people, but rather powerful private interests.

"This is a government of the interests, by the interests, and for the interests."

And so on ad nauseam.

Oregon complacently confronts the pessimists of the republic with startling statements somewhat as follows:

If our representatives do not represent us, we have power to force them to do so.

We can reject any law that we don't want, or ourselves enact any law that we do want.

We have knocked out boss and machine.

We have just elected two United States Senators in twenty minutes without "boodle or booze or even a cigar," and our legislature has just completed a session of extraordinary activity, untainted by any charge of corruption.

All of which, it may be acknowledged, indicates a condition of political wellbeing that justifies felicitation. And for such achievement the state may give thanks for the persistence of a small coterie, once laughed at by politicians as "Pops," "cranks" and "visionaries" led by a "dreamer."

The "dreamer" was W. S. U'Ren, who, a dozen years ago, was an obscure attorney in the little old village of Oregon City, where his sign is still displayed on the door of a very modest office.[3] U'Ren proved to be quite awake—a man of constructive genius and of such practical mind that he "cares less for means than for results"—where the latter are worthy of attainment. In fact, he and his associates demonstrated their ability to play the game of politics against veteran experts, and win.

Although the initiative and referendum amendment and the various measures which have arisen from it are the work of a considerable number, and although U'Ren emphatically denies that he is entitled to more credit than many others, yet the extraordinary character, the optimistic, persuasive personality and persistence of the man so dominates in the history of the movement for direct legislation that he is often playfully referred to as "Father U'Ren, of the Referendum."

George H. Williams
(c. 1875) [122]

George H. Williams, war-time Senator from Oregon and later Attorney-General in Grant's Cabinet, was the first to advocate direct legislation in this state. As a member of the Constitutional Convention of Oregon in 1857 he introduced a resolution embodying the essence of the measure which he has lived to see in operation fifty years later.

But the inception of the movement for the present law may be credited to the reading by Alfred Luelling of a chapter from J. W. Sullivan's *Direct Legislation in Switzerland* before a Farmers' Alliance meeting at Milwaukie, Oregon, late in the

[3]U'Ren began practicing law in Oregon in 1898; see Chapter 9—Ed.

Fall of 1892.[4] After the meeting, Mr. Luelling handed the book to W. S. U'Ren, one of the Alliance members present.

"I read the book through before I slept that night," Mr. U'Ren told me, "being already interested in the subject through reading a little pamphlet on the initiative handed me a year or so before by a man on a San Francisco Bay ferry."

At the next meeting of the Milwaukie Alliance, U'Ren introduced a resolution asking the state executive committee of the Alliance to invite the State Grange, the Portland Chamber of Commerce, the Oregon Knights of Labor (then a powerful organization) and the Portland Federated Trades to unite in creating a joint committee, consisting of one member from each body to "agitate and work for the adoption of the initiative and referendum" as a part of the Constitution of Oregon. The Alliance committee approved, sent out invitations, and appointed W. S. U'Ren as the Alliance member. The Portland Chamber of Commerce ignored the invitation. Some of the members have said that it was beneath the dignity of the body to mix up with any (expletived) Populist phantasm; others more considerately put it that the Chamber could take no part in politics. However, years afterward, the Chamber was glad to "mix up" to the extent of using the threat of the initiative as a club to stop a proposition of which it disapproved.

But the other organizations promptly appointed members to the joint committee. W. D. Hare, of the State Grange, was chairman. The Federated Trades Assembly of Portland was represented first by A. I. Mason, of the Carpenters' Union, next by G. G. Kurtz, of the Cigarmakers, and finally by Charles V. Short, of the Typographical Union. The Portland Labor Council by T. E. Kerby, of the Blacksmiths. The Knights of Labor were represented by W. S. Vanderburg. W. S. U'Ren was secretary.

These farmers and trades-unionists wrote folders and pamphlets

---

[4] *Direct Legislation by the Citizenship Through the Initiative and Referendum* [105]—Ed.

setting forth arguments for the initiative and referendum, and published them both in English and German. They also devised the plan of furnishing similar matter to newspapers in the form of supplements, which they induced editors to fold in with their publications for distribution to all readers. In this manner some 400,000 bits of propaganda were distributed by the committee throughout the state during the years from 1892 to 1898.[5] In the Fall of 1894, the committee having its campaign well under way, got up a petition, secured 14,000 signatures, representing every county in the state. This petition was presented to the legislature of 1895. It asked for a constitutional convention for the purpose, chiefly, of submitting to the people a new state constitution including the initiative and referendum. The Constitution then provided that two successive sessions of the legislature must pass a bill for an amendment before it could be submitted to the vote of the people. Therefore, if a constitutional convention could be obtained, the desired measure might be secured much quicker than by submitting it in the form of an amendment.

That the committee's bill failed by only one vote in either house, though encountering quite a strong lobby, indicates that the cranks and dreamers had already done very effective educational work. Some of the workers dropped out disgusted, but others with U'Ren kept on with undiminished resolution.

Populism, which flourished in those days, carried U'Ren into the legislature of 1897. As a member of the House he quickly took rank, in the judgment of us newspapermen at least, as the readiest debater and cleverest fighter on the floor.

That was the famous hold-up session. John H. Mitchell was candidate for re-election to the United States Senate,[6] but his

---

[5]Before the 20th century, the word 'propaganda' was a neutral descriptive term—Ed.

[6]John H. Mitchell (1835–1905) was a U.S. Senator from Oregon three times between 1873 and 1905—Ed.

"apostasy" on the silver question cost him the support of five "silver" Republicans, led by Jonathan Bourne,[7] candidate for speaker. These managed to form a coalition with thirteen Populists, three Democrats and nine "regular" Republicans, who were opposed to Mitchell "dictating the organization of the House in his own interests." This curiously constituted group managed, by preventing a quorum, to keep the House from organizing.

John H. Mitchell
(c. 1875) [119]

Now the thirteen Populists cared little for Mitchell or for the faction opposed to him. They were pledged to use their best efforts in behalf of certain reform measures, chief of which was the initiative and referendum, but being in hopeless minority could scarcely expect to accomplish much unless by finesse. Senator Mitchell was unquestionably the boss of the stronger Republican faction. One day before the session U'Ren sought to get his attitude upon the initiative and referendum. Mitchell stroked his beard and said in his characteristically gentle manner:

"I wouldn't introduce the bill if I were you; my friends won't support it."

Although Mitchell afterward denied that such was his real feeling, the Populists interpreted the remark as a clear indication of hostility to their pet measure. So when the anti-Mitchell leaders made overtures for their support, promising in exchange to take up and help forward, at the next legislative session (1899) not only the initiative and referendum, but the Bingham regis-

---

[7]Jonathan Bourne, Jr. (1855–1940) was elected to the U.S. Senate from Oregon in 1906. He served in that office from 1907 to 1913—Ed.

tration law (another important reform Oregon owes the Populists), the reformers saw their opportunity. Led by U'Ren and John C. Young, they hung together in a body under the banner of Jonathan Bourne, who afterward proved to be an enthusiastic and powerful friend to all their important measures. These men have been more or less bitterly assailed as being responsible for the hold-up, but it may be left to the judgment of the reader to decide whether the results they were striving for were not of as much value to the state as the temporary loss of a Senator or of such legislation as that boss-ridden session might have given it. "Anything to beat Mitchell" was sufficient excuse for the Democratic and Republican members of the coalition, and Mitchell was beaten for the time.

After the 1897 legislative session the enterprise dragged. The hard times had practically destroyed organized labor, so that of the four bodies, the Federated Trades Council, the Knights of Labor, the Farmers' Alliance and the State Grange, only the last survived. The Populists had fused with the Democratic party, but not all the ideals they had fought for were dead. U'Ren, C. C. Hogue, Jonathan Bourne and Frank Williams were practically the only ones left to keep up the fight for the initiative and referendum.

Jonathan Bourne, Jr.
(c. 1911) [33]

One Sunday in SEPTEMBER, 1897—weekdays could ill be spared for the work, for many of the reformers were poor men like U'Ren, who remarked that he didn't think the day could be put to better use—about fifty men met at Salem and organized "The Non-Partisan Direct Legislation League of Oregon," with D. C. Sherman as president, U'Ren being secretary. Thus a fresh start secured, the ball was kept rolling.

The previous legislature (1895) had by a deadlock also failed to re-elect a Senator (J. N. Dolph). As in many yet earlier sessions, legislation and all other business of the state body bad been interfered with, members corrupted, the state disgraced and some of our "sacred institutions" made more or less a mockery by the warring factions in Senatorial fights, and by the sinister dominance of private interests and boss influence.

The people of Oregon—"mossbacks" though they have been sometimes derisively styled—were becoming thoroughly disgusted. They were beginning to realize that some of our institutions are not entirely perfect. The operation of the Australian ballot law had taught them that other nations had something to offer in the way of improvement, and that America has no monopoly of progress; in fact, that by reason of its own self-conceit perhaps the nation had been at a standstill politically while other people were advancing. "What is this direct legislation these fellows are talking about? They say it works well in Switzerland. Well, Australia taught us something; perhaps Switzerland can also."

Thus the propaganda sowing of the "visionaries" was taking root. Their literature was of the model sort; simple, direct argument and example, appealing solely to the reason and to knowledge derived from experience; answering objections calmly, stating facts interestingly. Something of the genial persuasiveness of the smiling, blue-eyed, indomitable Oregon City lawyer ran through it all.

Here are two illuminating paragraphs from one of the pamphlets of the time—bits of advice addressed to those already converted and working for the reform:

> Do not urge a candidate to declare for or against the initiative and referendum as a system. If he will promise to submit the amendment, that is enough.

> If he is not convinced of its wisdom, it will be his duty to oppose it at the ballot box, as it is ours to advocate it.
>
> Let us show to the politicians of the United States, as well as those of Oregon, that support for the submission of direct legislation amendments is a sure way for the politician to get votes for himself—that party lines cut no figure on this question. Prove to the politicians that we are loyal and true at the ballot box to those who help us in the legislature.

Politicians paused to joke with U'Ren, or the other leaders, stayed to listen, and passed on, thoughtful. And the big men of the state, the brainy lawyers, broad-minded merchants, bankers, teachers and leading editors were also impressed. They began to talk; to make favorable speeches; to write friendly editorials. Then the movement really boomed. U'Ren and his friends of the committee seized upon every favorable speech or editorial and the name of every new convert as ammunition with which to load fresh propaganda.

H.W. Scott, editor of the Republican *Oregonian*, "sole avenue of publicity" of importance at that time, denounced the legislature and, on occasion, the machine, and at one or two critical stages of the fight presented arguments for direct legislation, which, says U'Ren, "aided us tremendously." The following is one of Mr. Scott's editorial expressions:

> The referendum is an obstacle to too much legislation; to surreptitious legislation; to legislation in particular interests; to partisan machine legislation, and to boss rule. No predatory measure could be carried before the people. The legislative lobbyist would be put out of business.

C. S. Jackson, for twenty years a fighter for political reform, now editor of the Portland *Journal*, the leading Democratic newspaper of the state, supported the movement with enthusiasm, and energetically worked for it as a member of the executive committee of the "Direct Legislation League." Nowadays *The Oregonian* and *Journal* vie with one another for the right to be considered the exclusive palladium of the people's rights.

C. E. S. Wood, a leader of the state bar, a man of radical, altruistic tendencies, and a writer of note, early became an advocate of the movement and performed invaluable service in the drafting of the bills for direct legislation and, in other ways, as a member of the league's executive committee.

An eloquent address, "About Direct Legislation," before the State Bar Association by the retiring president, Stephen A. Lowell (then Circuit Judge), in 1898, gave the movement another big boost. Among Judge Lowell's expressions were the following:

> Every effort thus far made to cure admitted evils of legislation has proven ineffectual because they have been movements away from the ideals of absolute freedom and complete popular control upon which the nation rests—movements away from the people, and not toward them.

> Briefly put, direct legislation is the inception and consummation of laws by the whole people—the substantial establishment of a pure democracy with Congress and legislature essentially the agents and not the masters of the people.

Leading business men also, convinced of the necessity for relieving the state from thralldom to politicians, began to study the measure, and, becoming convinced of its value and practicability, promptly endorsed it. W. M. Ladd and Charles E. Ladd, heads of the largest private banking enterprise of the West; A. L. Mills, president of the First National Bank of Portland, and many others of prominence throughout the state gave it hearty support.

It was soon after the organization of the Direct Legislation League that the movement sprang into giant stride. Judge George H. Williams, already mentioned as the pioneer advocate of the plan in Oregon, was persuaded to become president of the league (after the retirement of D. C. Sherman).

"I'm getting too old to take any active part," he said, but he quickly became one of the hardest workers; moreover the reformers found his name a tower of strength. To be identified with the enterprise was now generally recognized as an honor. Other names prominent on committees were George M. Orton, a printer and a fine type of trade-union man, who worked indefatigably for the reform; Dr. Harry Lane, a Democrat, now Mayor of Portland, of whom more will be said; Frank Williams, of Ashland, a man of tireless energy and enthusiasm; Former Governor T. T. Geer; Sol Hirsch, the most prominent Hebrew of the state; J. B. Waldo, D. K. Warren, F. E. Beach, F. McKercher, John C. Young, E. C. Pentland, W. A. Spaugh, J. C. Bayer, W. D. Hare of the old joint committee, and others.

All expenses were paid from voluntary contributions received from people of all parties and classes throughout the state. Whenever a deficit happened, the leaders always promptly went down into their pockets and made it up. Judging from some of the treasurer's old reports, I fancy that U'Ren must have indulged his "dreams" at some sacrifice of other luxuries.

Presently came the legislature of 1899, and with it some members pledged for the initiative and referendum. U'Ren and Frank Williams devoted their time working for the amendment during the entire session. The politicians were not unmindful of the powerful sentiment growing in the state; also they liked U'Ren and Williams; also the Simon contingent remembered the promises made the Populists during the session of 1897. The result was that the initiative and referendum bill got forty-four votes in the House and twenty-two votes in the Senate—an overwhelming majority and a tremendous surprise to many who yet affected to regard the measure as a "Pop fad."

But as, in accordance with the State Constitution, the amendment must be passed by two legislatures before it could be submitted for final test by vote of the people, the workers were by no means out of the woods. The amendment's enemies—a number of professional politicians and their friends, and a few large corporations that dreaded results, as well as many honest but timorous men who felt that the thing was too "revolutionary"—yet thought it would be blocked by the next legislature. But the initiative and referendum promptly became the one absorbing issue of the next campaign. The league redoubled its efforts on educational lines, members devoting many Sundays to this sort of practical religion. The whole state was studying and discussing the subject. U'Ren prepared a clever article, patting the late legislature on the back for its good work, and touching gently upon the evil that it had done, but suggesting how that evil could not have happened had the initiative and referendum been in operation. That astute reformer no doubt had heard something about more flies being caught with honey than with vinegar, but as a matter of fact U'Ren seems to be one of those rare persons quite anxious to give the devil his due with abundant interest of charity.

A little later in the campaign U'Ren selected the names of about 1,000 men, mostly ex-Populists, whom he knew, and addressed each a letter calling attention to the state legislators who had voted right in 1899, and who were again candidates, and suggesting that in the interest of the initiative and referendum it would be wise to support those men without regard to party. With the exception of Portland, where, as usual, was a bitter factional fight, no one of these candidates was defeated for re-election to the same office. John H. Mitchell was in power again and, grown wise by past experience, gave U'Ren assurance of his support this time; not only that, but added energetic action. The enemies of the measure were hopelessly beaten, and it went through the 1901 legislature almost unanimously. When the state conventions of 1902 were held, all except the Prohibitionists (strange as that may seem) adopted enthusiastic resolutions advocating the adoption of the initiative and referendum by the people. The Prohibitionists were afterward glad to make great use of the power secured for them.

So at last the people of Oregon got the chance to vote themselves into unlimited power. On JUNE 2, 1902, they declared themselves eleven to one for the amendment; and whether for good or for ill, it is a safe prediction that they will never vote that power back to the hands of the politicians. The actual vote was 62,024 for and 5,668 against, out of 92,920 total number of electors voting.

But the fight was not quite over; the last blow—almost a knock-out—came in the form of a decree of the Circuit Court for Multnomah County, which declared that the amendment had not been submitted in the manner required by law and was therefore void. The reformers promptly pulled off their coats again and carried the question up to the State Supreme Court. The lawyers who made the brief and argument in defense of the amendment contributed their services and paid all expenses from their own pockets. The Supreme Court sustained their contention, and thus finally the great reform was cleared of the last obstacle.

§ § §

Oregon is feeling its way carefully, polishing and whittling into handier form its big stick, and though there is no telling how far it will be taken, most of us in this state are optimists enough to believe that it can never be used long in any direction against the interests of the many, for it has the inherent power to correct its own misuse.

As for the "dreamer" and the "visionaries" who cut that stick from the forest of liberty and trimmed it into shape for Oregon, perhaps to their descendants they may bulk to the size of "constructive statesmen," and one day, a century hence, adorn in bronze effigy the public squares of some well-governed city yet to be.

Source: *The Pacific Monthly*—MAY 1907 [84]

2

U'REN LEADS A QUIET
REVOLUTION

NEXT, WE PRESENT AN ARTICLE from the JULY 1911 issue
of *McClure's Magazine* (1893–1929), a popular illustrated monthly that started the tradition of 'muckrak-
ing' journalism at the turn of the 20th century.

Burton J. Hendrick (1870–1949) wrote the piece. Besides being
an important journalist and 'muckraker', he also wrote books,
winning the Pulitzer Prize three times for: *The Victory of the Sea*
(History 1921), *The Life and Letters of Walter H. Page* (Biography
1923), and *The Training of An American* (Biography 1929).

Written four years after the Pease article presented in Chapter
1, Hendrick retells the story of how the people of Oregon came
to grant themselves the power of the Initiative and Referendum.
He shows how U'Ren, and other prominent Oregonians, used
politics to rid Oregon of corruption and inefficiency in public life by fundamentally modifying the representative system of
government.

Along the way, Hendrick reports on the small group of people who launched U'Ren on his crusade, the role of the Populist Party, U'Ren's background, Oregon's history, the problems with government as it worked then, and the actions and
roles of many of the people involved, on both sides, during the
ten-year campaign.

The Initiative and Referendum
and How Oregon Got Them
By Burton J. Hendrick

Nothing is more significant of the popular attitude toward political organizations than the movement, now rapidly spreading all over the United States, for the Initiative, the Referendum, and the Recall. Six Western State legislatures, in the last few months, have adopted constitutional amendments providing for these measures. The more conservative East, which a few years ago was ridiculing them as wild Populistic vagaries, is now beginning to give them respectful attention. How marked is the change in public opinion was evidenced only the other day, when Woodrow Wilson, for several years president of Princeton University, now Governor of New Jersey, and one of our leading academic authorities on politics and government, announced his conversion.

"For twenty years," said Governor Wilson, "I preached to the students of Princeton that the Referendum and Recall was bosh. I have since investigated, and I want to apologize to those students. It is the safeguard of politics. It takes power from the boss and places it in the hands of the people. I want to say with all my power that I favor it."

For the origin of this popular movement in the United States we must go back nearly twenty years, to a series of meetings held in an unpretentious farm-house in Milwaukie, Clackamas County, Oregon. The first inspiration had been given by a Reverend M. V. Rork, an ex-Unitarian clergyman, who came roaring through rural Oregon in the early '90's as the representative of the Farmers' Alliance. Rork was one of those Populistic agitators whom the Eastern newspapers so dearly loved to caricature; his lectures were directed against the railroads, Wall Street, and the existing political parties, and his favorite remedy was the combination of the farmers and the working classes against exploiting "capitalism." He made a business of organizing branches of the Farmers' Alliance, and with great success. In western Oregon, in particular, his progress was the heralding of a new political age.

Milwaukie, a village of perhaps a thousand people, located in one of the most fruitful sections of the beautiful Willamette Valley, about seven miles south of Portland, was the gathering-place of an energetic and intelligent yeomanry. Here the farmers thought and read and closely followed political movements and all important public questions. There was one family, in particular, which for many years had acted as an intellectual stimulus upon the town. Seth and Alfred Luelling were especially favorable specimens of rural Americanism—of the sturdy

Seth Lewelling
(c. 1890) [35]

and honest pioneers who had crossed the plains in ox teams and laid, in Oregon, the foundations of one of America's greatest commonwealths. They were prosperous nurserymen; they owned and cultivated several hundred acres; and, in their own profession, they are known as the creators of the famous "Bing" and "Luelling" cherries. But they were more than fruit-growers; they were natural philosophers: though academically uneducated, they had definite ideas on most religious, political, and economic questions. Almost inevitably their ideas were revolutionary. In religion they were spiritualists; Seth Luelling's house, indeed, was the local headquarters of spiritualism long before it became the meeting-place of political malcontents. The very room where the agitation for popular government in Oregon started had been for many years previously the scene of spiritualistic séances. Many of America's leading spiritualists

were the Luellings' intimate friends. Elizabeth Cady Stanton
had also visited the Luellings' home and had written from there
on questions concerning women.

A Group of "Advanced Thinkers"

Lewelling House C. 1933
DEMOLISHED IN 1940. [37]

The Luellings organized the Farmers' Alliance Lodge in Milwaukie,
and the Luelling farmhouse became its official headquarters.[1]
Here Seth and Alfred gradually
drew about them a philosophic
group and held weekly meetings for the discussion of current
events. All their associates belonged to the class known, in those
days, as "advanced thinkers." An
"advanced thinker" was usually
a man who declaimed vigorously
against the extortions of the railroads, who considered that both
political parties existed only to
serve the interests of corporate
wealth, who believed in the free coinage of silver at the ratio
of sixteen to one, and in the single tax. His chief idol among
public men was usually Henry George; his greatest aversion,
Grover Cleveland—Mr. Cleveland was then well launched in
his second term. The Luelling group represented certainly all
the forces of unrest that were soon to blossom into the Populist party—farmers' alliances, granges, knights of labor, labor-
unions, greenbackers, Socialists, and the rest. At one of these
Thursday evening meetings one could usually hear irreverently

[1]The frame building was designed and built to be a tavern by Elisha Kel-
logg in 1851. Seth Lewelling purchased it in 1852 and adapted it to be a
residence. Before it was demolished in 1940, it was located at 10966 SE
McLoughlin Blvd in Milwaukie, Oregon—Ed.

discussed nearly all the most sacred American institutions—the Supreme Court, the United States Senate, the representative system of government, even the Constitution itself. Many tenets then regarded as Socialistic—such as governmental ownership of railroads—likewise found hearty indorsement here. Women participated in the proceedings almost as generally is men; and one of the strongest articles of the Luelling faith—as it afterward became of the Populist party—was woman suffrage. The company frequently interrupted the political arguments with incursions into polite literature; they read and discussed good books; and one of the most entertaining members was a well-known Shakespearian "reciter," John D. Stevens.

William S. U'Ren

William S. U'Ren
(c. 1911) [35]

Cranky, irresponsible, half baked —all these things, in conservative eyes, the little assemblage certainly was; yet it was alive and stimulating. Out of this, and out of thousands of similar groups then scattered through the West, developed many of the ideas that have now reached the full dignity of practical politics. In the fall of the year 1892 the Luelling lodge admitted an important new member. This was a wanderer with a strange name—William Simon U'Ren.[2] Mr. U'Ren, like the Luellings, was a spiritualist, and, like most other spiritualists in that part of the country, he naturally gravitated toward the Luelling headquarters. He was then about thirty-two years old—tall, slender,

[2] Accent on the last syllable.

blue-eyed, yellow-haired, not in the best of health, but with an engaging manner, a ready tongue, and a quiet and deliberate interest in public questions. Although a young man, U'Ren had lived in many States and had acquired at first hand much political information. Radicalism he had breathed in as a child. His mother was a hardy Cornish woman; his father—still living and a Socialist at seventy-six—was an Englishman who, as a young man, had become dissatisfied with the political and social system of England, and had sought new ideals in this country. Here, as a blacksmith, he had prospered, but he had failed to find the equality and political morality of which he had dreamed. U'Ren's earliest recollections, as a child, were of fireside discussions of the land system in England; his father is still helping a brother in England to pay rent upon a house which their own grandfather built in the eighteenth century. There seemed something wrong in all this, but U'Ren could not quite understand where the fault lay.

The elder U'Ren had something of a library, in which William read as a boy; but his mother's reading of the Bible gave him his real education. "I was especially fond of the Old Testament leaders," he says, "Moses and the rest; I suppose it's because they were never satisfied with things as they were, but were always kicking." This training he supplemented by the usual course in the public schools of Colorado. Born in Wisconsin in 1859, he "vibrated," to use his own expression, for several years around the West, engaging in several occupations. He was, at various times, a blacksmith in the railroad yards at Denver, a bookkeeper, a shorthand writer, and a lawyer. He frequently took a hand in politics; he knew Colorado intimately, and here he first came into personal contact with political corruption. Going from one State to another—Colorado, Nebraska, Kansas, Iowa, California among others—he saw everywhere the same conditions, the same clear and simple system—the assumption of governmental powers by the forces of wealth. All these apparent facts, however, confused his mind. He saw no way out, no remedy. One day, in the mining camp of Tincup, Colorado, a friend handed U'Ren a book that had been recently written by a Californian. It was "Progress and Poverty." U'Ren's mind had already proved a receptive field for many revolutionary ideas; he was already a paper-money man; and in Henry George's work he found, or thought he found, a genuine political purpose in life. U'Ren has never been an agitator of the type frequently met with in the West—never a ranter, never ill-tempered, unreasonable, or dogmatic, but always soft-voiced, insinuating, persuasive, as good at listening as at talking. And now he brought all these gifts to bear in his missionary labors for the single tax. "Now I began to see why we were paying rent on a house our own grandfather had built in England a hundred years ago," he says; and it was this enthusiasm that he brought to the weekly gatherings at the Luelling household.

Oregon Hears of the Swiss System

He was a valuable acquisition. The reformers had been to a great degree inarticulate and purposeless, and in U'Ren they found their leader. He became a member of the Luelling household, and a partner with Seth Luelling in the nursery business. Hard times soon fell upon U'Ren, the Luellings, and all the

U'Ren's cabin in Milwaukie.
(c. 1911) [35]

rest of their associates. The panic of 1893 virtually ruined the orchard and nursery business, and financial gloom settled down upon Clackamas County. Farm products could not be sold; debts began to accumulate, farms to be mortgaged and foreclosed. U'Ren, who was at the time unmarried, lived in a little cabin on the Luelling estate. The philosophic group still held their weekly meetings, and constantly discussed their troubles. They could see only one cause for them—Wall Street, capitalism, the "money trust," the "railroad trust."

One evening Alfred Luelling brought to the gathering a copy of a new, paper-covered book. It was called "Direct Legislation by the Citizenship, through the Initiative and Referendum," and was written by J. W. Sullivan. Strange words, these—Initiative and Referendum. Several years before this, when he was crossing the ferry from San Francisco to Oakland, some one had handed U'Ren a labor-union circular on the "Initiative"; but hardly any other member of the group had heard of this governmental device. All were greatly interested, however, while Alfred Luelling read a few chapters to them. He could not finish the book at one reading, and after the meeting had adjourned, U'Ren took the volume and retired to his cabin. There, all night long, by the light of a little kerosene lamp, he pored over Sullivan's work. By sunrise he had read and digested every word.

"I forgot, for the time, all about Henry George and the single tax," he says. "All these I now saw to be details. The one important thing was to restore the law-making power where it belonged—into the hands of the people. Once give us that, we could get anything we wanted—single tax, anything."

Sullivan's teachings were radical because they proposed to modify seriously the fundamental, principle of American government. The men who framed the federal and the State constitutions unquestionably accepted, as a political maxim, the idea that democracy could work successfully only as long as the people ruled, not directly, but through elected representatives. They had no abiding confidence in an unrestrained democracy. Hamilton and his associates had constantly before them the historic failures—the Greek cities—in which the people exercised directly, in person, the law-making power. In the American Constitution, therefore, they separated as much as possible the lawmaking and the executive bodies from the people who elected them. Virtually all of the American States had followed the federal example. Oregon, in 1893, had such a representative system. This idea regulated every phase of its public life.

According to the representative idea, the rank and file could serve no useful purpose in making laws. They were a "mob." They were ignorant, capricious, unthinking, and were constantly led astray by their own passions. Could a "mob" vote upon laws—give a simple "yes" or "no" upon proposed measures of legislation? The suggestion, of course, was absurd. The one thing that the people could be trusted to do was, at stated intervals, to select, among the candidates proposed by the several political parties, the men who should make law-making their exclusive business. After selecting these representatives the voters lost all control of them. Such legislators simply ruled by royal ukase for the period for which they were chosen. If they did ill, the people had no recourse; they could not themselves undo their acts; they could not obtain the measures that their real interests demanded. Their only recourse was to wait until their representatives' terms had expired, and then elect a new set, who might go on betraying their trust precisely as had their predecessors. Under a properly regulated representative system such as the fathers of the Republic had foreseen, these things, of course, would never have happened. The men chosen by the people would be supremely wise and supremely good; they would be the State's leading men—its great educators and philanthropists, its honorable leaders in business, finance, professional life, arts and letters—men whose only possible motive in public life would be an unselfish interest in the public welfare.

Representative Institutions in the "Oregon Country"

Oregon had adopted a constitution, in 1859, founded upon this idea. How had it worked in practice?

This beautiful far-Western State apparently offered a fruitful field for such an idyllic experiment. Nature had endowed the soil with almost exhaustless wealth. The "Oregon country" is a lotus-eating land. Roses bloom in December, and crops burst out of the ground with the smallest amount of human labor. Almost tropical in its vegetative exuberance, it has nothing enervating in its climate. The women are robust, animated, alert;

the men, tall, ruddy-faced, bright-eyed, are extraordinarily energetic. In its settlement, Oregon drew upon many of the best elements in the American stock. The Western coast was settled largely by New Englanders, many of them seafaring people. There is a tradition that, when the time came to name their leading city, the pioneers tossed a coin to determine whether they should call it Portland or Boston; and Portland, to-day, with its central green, its general atmosphere of quiet respectability, strongly resembles a New England town. The State has always been mainly agricultural. Even now the population is only about seven hundred thousand.[3] Only one third live in the cities—the rest are found on the wheat farms, in the apple orchards and berry fields, on the lonely sheep and cattle ranches. Anglo-Saxondom is the largest element in its population, while its foreign population represents the better European peasant types—Irish, Scotch, Germans, and Scandinavians.

Here, if anywhere, this unmodified representative system, this full flower of Teutonic civilization, ought to bring happiness and justice to the people. A complete analysis, however, shows that in practically every branch of government it had been a humiliating failure. Even among American State governments, Oregon enjoyed a unique distinction for the corruption and inefficiency of its public life. It had a representative government, indeed, but not a government representative of its people. In 1893, when the Luellings, U'Ren, and the Milwaukie group began to reform the State, one could hardly say that popular government, in any real sense, existed at all. There was merely a skeleton—a hollow frame of representative institutions. The power that did select its representatives was made up of the corporations—the street railway, the gas and electric light companies, the banks, the railroads. With these had developed a kind of feudal aristocracy—the "first families of Portland"—which habitually used public powers for private ends.

[3]The population of Oregon in 1890 was 317,704; in 1900, 413,536; and in 1910, 672,765 [13]—Ed.

"Representatives" in Parties and Government

These several extra-constitutional powers had acquired possession of the government by using agencies the existence of which Hamilton and his associates had not foreseen. The fathers never seemed to anticipate, for example, the inevitable development of political parties. They provided that our representatives should be elected, but neglected an even more important detail—that, before being elected, they should be nominated. Under the representative system, the men who make the nominations clearly control the government. In Oregon, as elsewhere, an elaborate machinery had been devised for making these nominations. It was not direct; like the government itself, it was purely "representative." The fact that the people had themselves no immediate choice, but expressed their preferences through representatives chosen by other representatives whom the people themselves sometimes selected, gave them little interest or influence in the proceedings. Thus there grew up a professional class which made a business of working this party machinery.

Oregon's "Wisest" and "Best"

In character the representatives thus selected fell far short of the Hamiltonian ideal. There were thousands of splendid, honest, able, patriotic gentlemen in Oregon—but they were not found, except rarely, in the legislature. Instead, there were briefless lawyers, farmless farmers, business failures, bar-room loafers, Fourth-of-July orators, political thugs. The larger part of these men were ignorant, illiterate, lazy, politically and personally immoral. As soon as the legislature convened, a troop of prostitutes quite regularly encamped at Salem—the law-makers, in some cases, attaching them to the State pay-roll. Drunkenness and debauchery commonly prevailed throughout the whole legislative session. These legislators organized in the interest of the corporations; the latter named the officers and the committees, and directed legislation.

How Switzerland had Driven the "Interests" Out of Politics

With Luelling, U'Ren, and the other members of the Milwaukie group, these conditions had for some time formed the staple of discussion. The reformers made little practical headway, however, until they read and pondered Sullivan's book and other literature of the same kind. Sullivan's volume described how, thirty or forty years before, essentially the same conditions had prevailed in Switzerland. There also, in that pastoral Republic, the "interests" had annexed the government, and had used it to increase their wealth. They were just about the same kind of interests that were exploiting Oregon—the railroads, the banks, the "plutocracy," and the corrupt politicians. There, too, there had been political machines and political bosses; legislatures had been corrupt and bribery had been common. In seeking a way of escape, a small group of Swiss reformers, in the '30's and '40's, began to advocate a general system of popular law-making. For centuries six Swiss cantons—Uri, Glarus, and the double cantons of Appenzell and Unterwalden—have been pure democracies. Here, once a year, usually on a Sunday in May, the mountaineers gather in the meadow, pass laws by a show of hands, and exercise in person all the functions of government. These *Landsgemenden,* the direct descendants of the Teutonic folkmoots, had long been an object lesson to the Swiss people. The writings of their celebrated philosopher, Rousseau, always an advocate of legislation directly by the people, had also become a part of the national political consciousness.

The cantons in which the *Landsgemeinde* ruled, however, were small, and the town-meeting idea was obviously impracticable in sections where the population reached into the tens of thousands. The reformers, therefore, originated what was essentially a new scheme. They provided for the retention of their representative chambers, and arranged that these chambers should still have charge of legislation. They simply reserved to the people two powers, one to pass laws themselves, the other to veto any obnoxious law passed by the legislature. The first power they called the Initiative, the second the Referendum. In several cantons all laws, before they became effective, had to be indorsed by a majority of the voters; in others, the acts of the legislature became laws without submission, unless a certain percentage of the freemen petitioned for a popular vote.

Sullivan's book, as well as many others written upon the same subject, claimed for these new measures unqualified success. Practically all the abuses that had prevailed under the former system had disappeared. Public life had become orderly and decent; the cantonal legislatures had ceased their turmoils and become honest and businesslike; bribery and corruption had disappeared; and in all its branches Switzerland, which had been one of the worst governed countries in Europe, had gradually become one of the best. Many great national reforms had been instituted. The State, instead of being owned by the railroads, now controlled these corporations—in recent years the government has actually owned them. Switzerland regulated the liquor traffic by making alcohol a State monopoly. The people had obtained an equitable system of taxation, had voted large appropriations for building highways and for other public purposes. Above all, the Swiss people had developed a new political sense, had a keen interest in public affairs, and kept fruitful watch over their legislatures. Unquestionably, at times they had made mistakes; but that the new system was of immense value, on the whole, seemed to be the judgment of nearly all who had investigated it.

A Movement of the Farmers and Working Classes

The Luelling group now began what developed into a ten years' agitation. They soon founded a definite organization—a "Joint Committee on Direct Legislation." They invited the State Grange, the Oregon Farmers' Alliance, the Portland Federated Trades, the Portland Central Labor Council, and the Oregon Knights of Labor to send delegates to discuss ways and means of getting the Initiative and Referendum. In order to make the meeting representative, they sent a similar invitation to the Portland Chamber of Commerce. All except the latter body accepted. The meeting was held in U'Ren's cabin on the Luelling estate. Although the popular movement in Oregon is now comprehensive, in that representatives of all social classes are supporting it, this preliminary meeting emphasizes distinctly that in the early days it was confined to the farming and the wage-earning class. Among the most active of the delegates were A. I. Mason, then a leader in the Carpenters' Union and afterward a letter carrier; George M. Orton, a printer; G. G. Kurtz, a cigar-maker; T. E. Kirby, a representative of the Knights of Labor; Nathan Pierce, president of the Oregon Farmers' Alliance; and W. D. Hare, from the State Grange. Nearly all of these men were familiar with the Initiative and Referendum in their own organizations—for years it had been their regular way of making laws. Unquestionably they regarded the reform as the most effective way of redressing their grievances—what they looked upon as the oppression of "capital."

This little band decided to strive for one thing—a convention for the revision of the Constitution, this revision to provide for the Initiative and Referendum. A change that would give legislative power to the voters necessarily required a change in this fundamental instrument.

Many Swiss and New Englanders in Clackamas County

For some time the seat of war was Clackamas County. Here the reformers found conditions favorable to their demands. The county is one of the most beautiful and prosperous in the State, and its people are unusually industrious and intelligent. Fortunately for the proposed reform, a considerable part of its population is German-Swiss. In Milwaukie where the movement started, at least half of the population are Swiss. These settlers brought with them many memories of popular law-making in their fatherland; they could remember the days when, after church on Sunday, they used to assemble on the village green, and, by uplifted hands, pass their own laws and select their own rulers.[4] Another considerable element in the population were New Englanders. With them, also, law-making by the people was not revolutionary or strange; for generations the freemen of the New England towns had met annually in town meetings, laid their own taxes, made their own appropriations, and chosen their own "selectmen." Naturally, these two classes of citizens, the Swiss and the New Englanders, needed little instruction; they eagerly fell into line to educate their less experienced neighbors.

Women Active in the Movement

The movement was a popular one in every sense of the word. In view of present-day discussions of the fitness of women for public affairs, it is interesting to note that, in accomplishing this the most revolutionary governmental change in the last half century, women played a conspicuous part. As a preliminary step, U'Ren and his associates issued a pamphlet discussing the proposed constitutional reforms—a small document that ultimately had a circulation of fifty thousand copies in English and fifteen thousand in German.

Sophronia V. Luelling.
(C. 1911) [35]

They had little money, and everybody, men, women, and children, had to help. The printers' unions did the printing; the women did the stitching; the children did their part in the

---

[4]Less than 20% of the population of Milwaukie, Oregon were Swiss. In 1890, 907 people lived in Milwaukie. The number of native-born Swiss in Clackamas County, population 15,233, which included Milwaukie, was 188 people—Ed [13] [29].

distribution. In the winter of 1894–95 nearly every farmer household in Milwaukie spent its evenings in this work. Several women took to the stump. Mrs. Sophronia Luelling, Seth Luelling's wife, was especially influential as a speaker at meetings of the Alliance and the Grange. A number of young school-teachers traveled over the country, addressing meetings in school-houses. Miss Florence Olsen was most active in this work. It had been the custom to hold social gatherings in these school-houses, at which the people turned out in families; the farmers' wives prepared the supper, and the evening was spent in discussing matters affecting their personal welfare. These gatherings brought together just the crowds desired: there were no politicians—there were only the people. Miss Olsen and her associates made a business of attending these functions and discussing the "I and R," the discussions being invariably followed by debate. Both men and women supplemented these discussions by personal appeals. They canvassed the whole country: John D. Stevens traveled on foot all over Clackamas County, carrying the gospel to every farm-house. All this time Sullivan's book was doing excellent service; thousands of copies were printed and circulated through the State, and each thumbed copy made the round of many farm-houses.

Florence Olsen.
(c. 1911) [35]

Together with their exhortations the campaigners circulated a petition humbly requesting the sovereign legislature of Oregon to call a constitutional convention. They obtained fifteen thousand signatures, all of voters, out of a total electorate of eighty thousand. They also took pains to pledge as many candidates as possible to vote for such a bill. When the legislature of 1895 convened, U'Ren, who had established his headquarters in the State Capitol, believed that he had pledged votes enough to pass the bill. But the predominant Republican machine energetically opposed it. It is significant of the change in

Oregon's public life that the most ferocious enemy of the reform in the session of 1895 was Judge Henry E. McGinn, who is at present one of the leaders in the popular movement. But Mr. McGinn was then merely the Senate leader of the Republican machine.

The Legislature Breaks Its Pledge

U'Ren haunted the legislature day and night, gently buttonholing members in the interest of his proposed convention. Few law-makers understood what he was talking about, but they all liked him for his mild manner and his amiable persistence. But he didn't make any headway with the legislature. In fact, many members who had pledged themselves to support the bill ostentatiously voted against it. It was perhaps just as well that they did. At that time U'Ren and his followers demanded a compulsory Referendum—a constitutional change requiring that all laws, before becoming valid, should receive the popular indorsement. Such a plan was impracticable, as the reformers soon decided. When they next appeared in public, therefore, they asked merely for the Referendum in its optional form—a provision that laws passed by the legislature should be submitted when eight per cent of the voters petitioned for such submission. They had also abandoned the idea of a constitutional convention, and merely asked for an amendment to the constitution providing for their reform.

The part that U'Ren played in the next session, that of 1897, clearly demonstrated that he had developed political talents of his own.

Reform Indirectly a Result of Senator Mitchell's Free-Silver Policy

Much political history had been made in these two intervening years. The free-silver issue, which had so completely demoralized and disrupted political parties in the other Western States, had played havoc in Oregon. Indirectly it was the means of giving Oregon its popular laws. For many years Senator John H. Mitchell had been the leading politician in the State. No man in Oregon's history has ever aroused so strong a popular enthusiasm; even to-day, in spite of Mitchell's miserable and disgraceful end,[5] the average Oregonian will defend his memory. The outsider, who has never succumbed to Mitchell's personal influence and knows him only by the facts of his career, cannot quite understand the affection in which he is still held. Mitchell spent his early days as a school-teacher in Pennsylvania, under the name of John M. Hipple, and went to Oregon in 1860. From the first he was successful in politics. He had the personal graces that count for everything in a young community—good looks, amiability, generosity, force, and a certain dash and aggressiveness that passed for intellectual brilliancy. He early associated himself as a lawyer and political adviser with Ben Holliday, a Kentucky stage-driver, who first began building railroads in Oregon. A remark attributed to Mitchell—"Ben Holliday's politics are my politics and what Ben Holliday wants I want"—sums up his system of political morals. Mitchell early formed a law partnership with Joseph N. Dolph, and in the late '60's took into his office, first as a law student and afterward as a clerk and partner, Mr. Joseph Simon—of whom more will be heard. For many years this law firm was virtually the governmental headquarters of the State—managed Republican politics, ruled the State legislature, and made and unmade United States senators. In the course of thirty years four members of this firm went to the United States Senate. Up to 1892 it not only dominated the State politically, but acted as counsel to the Southern Pacific Railroad. For many years its junior member, Joseph Simon, has been the officially recognized head of the State machine.

Mitchell's third term in the United States Senate was to expire

[5]In 1905, Mitchell, while a sitting Senator, was indicted and convicted in Oregon's land fraud scandals—Ed.

on MARCH 4 1897. In the campaign of the preceding fall—the Presidential gold-silver campaign of 1896—his reelection had figured extensively as an issue. Up to the time of McKinley's nomination, Mitchell had been the leading free-silver Republican in Oregon. His speeches on this subject in the Senate had been uncompromising, had received wide publicity, and had unquestionably strengthened his chances of reelection to the Senate. In those days State elections took place in June, and consequently Mitchell adherents to the legislature had been chosen before the national Republican convention had met and before any weakening in Mitchell's free-silver advocacy had become known.

Jonathan Bourne, of New Bedford

Mitchell's campaign manager in 1896 was another Republican aggressively in favor of free silver—one of the most remarkable men in the State, Jonathan Bourne, at present senior United States senator from Oregon. All his life Bourne had feasted on excitement and adventure. He was born in New Bedford, in 1855, of wealthy parents. He spent three years at Harvard, but left college to go to sea. The voyage proved to be an exciting and memorable one; Bourne cruised for a time around China, was wrecked off Formosa, and was finally picked up and carried to Portland, Oregon. This was about 1880, and Portland was then a small town with not more than forty thousand people.[6] Bourne liked it, and decided to stay. He read law and was admitted to the bar, but did not practise extensively. It was inevitable that a man with Bourne's activity and interest in life should take a hand in politics, for politics, in those days, furnished the chief entertainment for young men in Oregon. He unquestionably had brains, much masterfulness in handling men, great intensity, and, with it all, remarkable energy and aggressiveness. He was subject to sudden enthusiasms, and, while

[6]In 1880, Portland's population was 17,577; in 1890, it was 46,385 [13]—Ed.

the spell lasted, was absolutely impenetrable to other interests. But Bourne did not make much headway because of what his enemies called his "destructive" tendencies. He accepted, as a matter of course, the prevailing political morals—that there could be any other way of doing things had not at that time occurred to him. But his fondness for "smashing things," his disinclination to play any game according to established rules, accounted for the distrust in which he was held by the machine leaders.

Bourne Elects a Mitchell Legislature

In 1896 Bourne had been seized by one of those engrossing enthusiasms to which he was subject. This time it was free silver. He himself had interests in silver-mines; in spite of this, his belief was undoubtedly sincere, and he certainly clung to it more consistently than did many of his associates. Indeed, all through the exciting time of 1896, he thought of nothing else, and talked of nothing else, but the crime of '73.[7] His management of Mitchell's campaign illustrates the methods of electing United States senators that then prevailed in Oregon. Bourne had the handling of Mitchell's campaign fund, and advanced expenses to the Republican candidates for the legislature. In turn, he pledged these candidates to vote for Senator Mitchell. Bourne did not do this in any half-hearted manner; he tied these men up in writing—drawing up documents that had all the external appearance of contracts. Bourne himself was elected to this legislature from Portland, and the agreement made between himself and Mitchell was that he was to be made Speaker of the House.

Mitchell Changes His Free-Silver Views and Drops Bourne

Long before the legislature convened, however, Mitchell had changed his position on the financial issue. He altered his views

[7] The Coinage Act of 1873—Ed.

to correspond with the gold plank in the national platform. Instead of being the great champion of the silver cause in Oregon, he was denounced from one end of the State to the other as a "gold-bug." Mitchell did not attempt to conceal the reason for this turn-about; the federal administration had informed him that no silver man could be elected senator from Oregon. And, in order to carry out the program in full, Mitchell also had to turn against Bourne, the man who had made his election absolutely certain. In the presidential campaign Bourne had supported Bryan—a course that, in Mitchell's view, made him unavailable as the Speaker of a Republican Assembly.[8] In fact, Mitchell believed that he would lose several votes if Bourne received this office.

Harvey W. Scott, the Pacific Coast Greeley

There were still further complications. Joseph Simon, who became President of the Senate, was then engaging in one of his periodical feuds against his old law partner, Mitchell. He was working hard for Mitchell's defeat, and ostensibly for the election of a rich Portland banker, ex-Senator Henry W. Corbett. Another power hostile to Mitchell was Harvey W. Scott, the brilliant editor of the Portland *Oregonian*. Scott was an old-fashioned journalist, whose activities were by no means confined to his editorial sanctum. In fact, for many years he had been one of the dictators of the Republican party in Oregon. As

Joseph Simon
(c. 1900) [88]

a newspaper man, Scott had a hold upon the respect and affection of the farmers in the North Pacific region comparable only

[8]William Jennings Bryan (1860–1925) was the Democratic Party's nominee for President of the United States in 1896, 1900, and 1908—Ed.

to that held, in the '50's and '60's, by Horace Greeley in the North Atlantic and Middle Western States. "What does old man Scott say?" was the first question asked by the average Oregon farmer, as each new issue came up for discussion. Born in Illinois in 1838, Scott had come to Oregon in 1852, traveling over the plains with an ox-team. As a boy he had helped to build a home in the wilderness—felling trees, working in sawmills and in the open fields, spending his evenings over the few books the pioneer household provided—the Bible, Shakespeare, and Milton. He lived these early days at his father's farm near Olympia, on Puget Sound; and at nineteen, after serving two years in a bloody Indian war, he heard of the establishment of an educational institution at Forest Grove, Oregon, under the pretentious title of the Pacific University. That was a long way off, in those days; there were no railroads or stage-coaches; but Scott made a bundle of the few books and clothes he possessed, threw them across his back, and started on a long tramp.

The country was so primitive that he had to swim across the Columbia and the Willamette rivers. When he passed through Portland, the city in which his great journalistic triumphs were afterward to be won, it was a straggling, muddy village. He walked fifty miles a day, ultimately reached the "university," and became its first graduate. This training and the studious habits of a lifetime made Scott an excellent scholar,—a good Latinist, fond of a daily dip into his

Harvey W. Scott
(c. 1903) [10]

Horace and Virgil, an expert in philosophy and theology, and well read in history, economics, and English literature. He became editor of the *Oregonian* in 1865, when it was a feeble broadside, and soon made it the one great intellectual newspaper of the Pacific States. Scott's editorial style was keen, stinging, Dana-esque, full of epigrams and pointed quotation, having a literary finish strangely out of keeping with his rude frontier environment. Judged by modern journalistic standards, however, Scott had many limitations. He had little real independence; he was constantly taking a hand in politics; and he judged most public men and public questions from a purely personal standpoint. His usefulness was injured by the consuming ambition of his life—his desire to represent Oregon in the United States Senate. The politicians constantly played upon this ambition, and cajoled Scott many times into supporting unworthy men and unworthy causes. At certain critical times, however, Scott's personal convictions rose superior to these influences, and one of these occasions was this campaign of 1896. He threw all of his energies into the gold-standard fight, and was the chief power in saving Oregon for a sound currency. This explains his hostility to the reelection of Mitchell—the man who had so ignominiously eaten his own words on this issue.

Certainly here was a remarkable legislative situation. Mitchell had enough pledged votes to secure reelection to the Senate. Bourne had been dropped by Mitchell and was now exerting all his energies to accomplish his defeat. Simon, the State boss, was working in the interest of another candidate, and Scott, also powerful politically, would go to almost any extreme to punish Mitchell and retire him to private life.

Who could possibly turn such a situation to any public good? There was one man who saw in it his opportunity—a chance to accomplish a cherished reform. That was William S. U'Ren.

Mitchell Opposed Initiative and Referendum

U'Ren had his own grievance against Senator Mitchell. In the course of the campaign of 1896, U'Ren had sounded Mitchell on the Initiative and Referendum. "Yes," said Mitchell, "that's all right—I think that amendment should be submitted."

U'Ren and his associates, therefore, regarded Mitchell as pledged to their reform. His support, indeed, was almost indispensable. In this same election U'Ren himself was chosen to the legislature from Clackamas County, as a Populist. All the farmers, with their wives and children, turned out, and, although the section had been overwhelmingly Republican for years, carried him into the legislature by a large majority. In the campaign U'Ren supported Bryan and free silver, but he talked of little except the Referendum. Sixteen Populists were elected, all pledged to this amendment; and of these U'Ren at once became the leader. In this capacity, after the election, he called upon Mitchell at his home—to make sure that he was still friendly to the cause.

"Well, Senator," he began, "I congratulate you; you certainly will be reelected."

"Oh, yes," replied Mitchell, "I have three Pops you can't take away from me."

"And I suppose you will help us get the Initiative and Referendum?"

"Hum!"—and Mitchell glanced down on the floor and stroked his patriarchal white beard. "If I were you, I don't think I would introduce that this session."

Mitchell afterward denied that he had intended, by these words, to notify U'Ren that he would not support the amendment; but U'Ren and his associates certainly so understood him. Mitchell's corporation allies, they believed, had forbidden any such revolutionary legislation. Two years before, a majority in the legislature had pledged themselves to the measures, and then had remorselessly broken their pledges. And now once more the farce was to be reenacted.

In order to understand subsequent events, one must clearly understand U'Ren's attitude toward the existing governmental system. If we are to indorse his legislative methods, we shall have to revise considerably our political morals. In discussing that famous session of 1897, U'Ren makes no attempt to conceal the facts and exculpate himself; he simply played the game, he says, according to the prevailing rules, and used such methods as he found ready to his hand.

"Politics," he says, "is war"; and at that time he was engaged not only in a war, but in a revolution. He had absolutely no respect for the existing political institutions; the State of Oregon was owned bodily by property interests and corporations; U'Ren and his followers were rebels—their one aim was to destroy this system and restore the governmental powers to the people. As, in war, the general's business is to grasp every opportunity, with not too scrupulous a regard for the rules that regulate everyday social intercourse,—to employ spies, to lay mines, to deceive,—so in this revolutionary uprising U'Ren believed that any methods were justifiable, provided only they succeeded. "For many years," says U'Ren, "I had seen reformers go in, and, using reform methods, accomplish nothing. I had tried to get the Initiative and Referendum in a respectable way twice—once in 1895 and here again in 1897. Both times our representative legislators had deceived and betrayed us. I now decided to get the reforms by using our enemies' own methods—by fighting the devil with fire."

The present writer makes no attempt to defend U'Ren's attitude; he wishes merely to explain it. The ethics of the procedure each one must settle for himself.

U'Ren Plays Upon the Weaknesses of Politicians

U'Ren clearly understood one important point: that politicians are invariably opportunists, and look upon important public movements only as they affect their immediate personal interest. His experience with the present agitation had taught him that. He now proceeded to play upon this common trait. He could get nothing out of Mitchell; if he was to succeed at all, he must work with Bourne, Simon, Scott, and the other anti-Mitchell men. The situation, as he saw it, was simple enough.

What did he want most of all from that legislature? The passage of the Initiative and Referendum amendment. What did Bourne, Simon, and the others desire above everything else? The defeat of Mitchell as United States senator. U'Ren's plan, therefore, was to make an offensive and defensive alliance with the anti-Mitchell element. If they would pledge themselves to help along his reform, he and his Populist following would pledge themselves to help defeat Mitchell.

In other words, U'Ren and Jonathan Bourne made a "deal." But it was a "deal" rather difficult to carry out. Mitchell had his votes all pledged; and the remarkable feature of the situation was that Bourne himself had secured these pledges. When the legislative hangers-on first heard of the arrangement, therefore, they simply laughed. As soon as the legislature convened and organized, they said, its first act would be to elect Mitchell United States senator.

Bourne and U'Ren acknowledged that this was entirely true. That was precisely the reason, they added, why the legislature was not going to organize—unless it could organize in their way.

Machinery of Government Stops in Oregon

When the time came for law-making, the Oregon Senate came to order, permanently organized, elected Joseph Simon President, and prepared for business. But in the House matters went more slowly. The body organized temporarily, but got no further. Instead it split into two practically equal parts. One part was composed of Republicans strongly favoring the reflection of United States Senator Mitchell. This organized as a rump assembly, but had no quorum, and so could do no business. Joseph Simon, as President of the Senate, steadily refused to recognize the body as the lower house. The second part was composed of nine Simon Republicans, five silver Republicans, three Democrats, and thirteen Populists. Jonathan Bourne led the Republican and Democratic insurgents, while William S.

U'Ren commanded the Populists. This second group declined to associate with the first. It would not go into the House and help organize; it would not go into caucus to choose a United States senator its members would not even take their oath of office. They made no secret of their motives. They sent emissaries to the regulars, proposing conditions upon which they would assume their constitutional functions. These were:

First: That Senator Mitchell should not be returned to Washington, but that some candidate satisfactory to the Simon wing should be chosen.

Second: That Jonathan Bourne should be elected Speaker of the House.

Third: That the Legislature should pass the Initiative and Referendum amendment, a registration law, and other remedial legislation.

Thus all elements in the insurrectionary band were to receive a *quid pro quo*. And they made a solemn compact to hold together. Unless the Mitchell people accepted these terms, there would be no legislative session that year.

Of course, Mitchell did not capitulate; and there followed probably the most disgraceful episode in the whole history of American legislatures. In Oregon the wheels of government ceased to turn; law-making stopped, no appropriation bills were passed, the ordinary routine of State business came to an end. Forty years of corruption in the legislature had reached a logical outcome in anarchy. In order to reform the State government on a new basis, U'Ren had abolished the old system. For forty days—the length of the session in Oregon—the law-makers hung around the bar-rooms, or sat listlessly on the Capitol steps, spitting tobacco juice and swapping stories. To provide them with entertainment, Bourne fitted up elaborate personal headquarters in Salem. When he ran for the United States Senate, in 1906, Bourne issued a pamphlet in which he described this establishment in detail:

"Those who were in the Bourne headquarters almost every day say," reads this pamphlet, "that Mr. Bourne rented all the available rooms in the Eldridge block, in Salem, hired two cooks and a waiter, fitted up a kitchen and dining-room, and entertained his friends as he would if they were guests at his own home. Two or three of his closest political friends made his quarters their home while in Salem. Others who had rooms elsewhere were frequent visitors at his headquarters and were often guests at his table. His steward supplied the table with the best the markets afforded, and every visitor who came was royally entertained."

On the whole, the Bourne-U'Ren combination succeeded. Bourne accomplished his main purpose—Mitchell's defeat. He did not obtain the Speakership: nor did anybody else; and on this score Bourne was satisfied. Simon had also defeated Mitchell; and, at the special session called next year to elect a United States senator, Simon himself received the prize, U'Ren did not get his Initiative and Referendum amendment that year, but he did receive the promises of his allies that at the next legislature it would go through.

And they kept their word. When a new legislature convened in 1899, one of its first acts was the passage of the resolution calling for the submission of this amendment. It was adopted by a large majority. Senator Mitchell had learned his lesson. For breaking his pledges to U'Ren two years before he had lost a United States senatorship. He still aspired to reelection, and he now respected U'Ren's ability and power.

Just before the session of 1901 opened, U'Ren—precisely as, four years before, he had sounded him on the proposed reform.

"You and I have had some troubles, Senator," U'Ren began.

Mitchell raised his hand in gentle deprecation.

"That's right, U'Ren," he said; "we *have* had troubles. But they are all in the past. If we have any more they'll be in the future. My friends will help you to get your Referendum through."

Two years after the legislature had adopted the Referendum a-mendment, Mitchell was reelected, for his fourth term, to the United States Senate.

By this time the movement had become respectable. The Populist party was dead; U'Ren himself had failed of election to the Senate in 1898; but the Initiative and Referendum had survived. The Oregon Constitution, however, was rather difficult to amend. The legislature had to pass an amendment at two succeeding sessions before it could be submitted to the people. U'Ren organized a Direct Legislation League, and succeeded in getting into it some of the "leading citizens" of the State—bankers, big merchants, and the like. Even W. D. Fenton, one of the counsel to the Southern Pacific Railroad, contributed fifty cents to the cause. All political parties, except the Prohibitionist, indorsed the innovation in their State conventions and Harvey W. Scott supported it in the Oregonian. The a-mendment, therefore, went smoothly through two different legislatures, and came up for popular indorsement in the election of 1902. There was a feeling, among certain pessimists, that the people would vote it down—constitutional amendments always seemed to fail in Oregon. They did not understand, however, the popular demand for this change. It was the custom in those days for candidates to distribute cards containing their pictures and declaration of principles, and in the election of 1902 one candidate shrewdly printed on his card, in red ink: "Vote for the Initiative and Referendum amendment." This advice made him so popular that virtually all the others followed his example. That the people of Oregon really demanded this law-making power was shown when the ballots were counted.

The amendment had been adopted by a vote of eleven to one, and, in this quiet revolution, political power in Oregon had been transferred from the bosses and the corporations to the citizenship.

Source: *McClure's Magazine*—JULY 1911 [35]

II

A MUCKRAKER IN OREGON

3

U'REN MEETS STEFFENS

ONE OF THE MOST FAMOUS JOURNALISTS at the beginning of the 20th century was Lincoln Steffens (1866–1936). He traveled the country looking for malfeasance, graft, and corruption in government and big-business. In 1907, he came to the Pacific Coast to find and write 'muckrakering' stories for *The American Magazine*.[1] One of those stories would be about William S. U'Ren.

Steffens was in Oregon from mid-MARCH to mid-APRIL 1907. His visit attracted the attention of the local press. This chapter will acquaint the reader with some of the newspaper stories published about him at that time.

Steffens arrived in Portland on 13 MARCH 1907. The next day, a Thursday, *The Morning Oregonian* noted Steffens' arrival:

LINCOLN STEFFENS HERE

Famous Reformer Comes to Gain First-Hand Information on Graft.

Lincoln Steffens, the distinguished magazine journalist and specialist on graft disclosure, is in Portland for the purpose of

[1]For Steffens' account of his trip, see Chapter 27 of *The Autobiography of Lincoln Steffens* [100]—Ed.

investigating the workings of Oregon's revolutionary political methods, the land frauds, with possibly some side excursions into the railroad situation. With Mrs. Steffens, he is a guest at the Portland Hotel, and will remain some considerable time. Subsequently Mr. Steffens will embody the results of his observations into one or more articles for the American Magazine, of which he is one of the owners and editors.

Source: *The Morning Oregonian*—14 MARCH 1907 [53]

One day later, on Friday, 15 MARCH, the *Oregon City Enterprise* ran a front-page story that revealed Steffens had been in Oregon City to interview the subject of this book, W. S. U'Ren:[2]

LINCOLN STEFFENS VISITS THIS CITY

Famous Graft Exposer Was in Town and Talks of His Mission To Oregon and What He Expects to Find

LOOKS UP GOOD AND BAD POINTS OF OREGON

Was in Oregon City as Guest of W. S. U'Ren to Talk over Initiative and Referendum and Other Reform Measures—Interested in Local Affairs.

[2] Oregon City is fifteen miles southeast of Portland, alongside the Willamette River—Ed.

"I haven't found any graft in Oregon City," said Lincoln Steffens, the famous graft exposer, to THE STAR last night.

Mr. Steffens arrived in Portland yesterday morning and yesterday afternoon was in Oregon City to talk with W. S. U'Ren on the initiative and referendum and kindred topics.[3]

There is probably no better known writer in the country than Lincoln Steffens on the subject of graft as an economic factor. He is famous for his exposures of Milwaukee, St. Louis, Philadelphia and other graft centers, and has wielded his muckrake unsparingly in the interest of reform in government. Wherever he goes it is expected that his mission is to dig up corruption in politics and government, and by the aid of publicity which his forceful pen can give, to help remedy the evils. At present he is editor-in-chief of the American magazine, the policy of which is for reform.

Why He Is Here.

Influenced by the general impression that obtains as to Mr. Steffens' work, the first question put to him was in regard to his mission to Oregon and what scandal he expected to unearth.

"I am making a tour of the west in the interest of my magazine," replied Mr. Steffens. "I have never worked before further west than Denver, and I wanted to come out to the Coast and become familiar with conditions out here."

Mr. Steffens mentioned his trip to California, speaking of the recall, or the power of the people to remove from office any man who is deemed incompetent or unfit to hold the office to which he has been elected.

[3]U'Ren's father and mother were living in Gladstone, Oregon, next to Oregon City. Steffens could have also interviewed them about their son.—Ed.

Sometimes Writes Good Things.

"In Los Angeles this power has been used but once," he said. "The law is in operation in Los Angeles, Pasadena, and other California towns, and it has been found that the existence of this power of the people has been sufficient. Where it can be used, it seldom has to be."

Lincoln Steffens.
(c. 1900) [3]

Mr. Steffens will observe the workings of the initiative and referendum and other reform measures which are in operation in Oregon.

"From my work in the past," he said, "people think I have no other object than to dig up graft and expose it. My interest in graft is only as it is an element in the corruption of government. Graft is a study by itself has no interest for me. I shall go into your land frauds because they present features of graft connected with the government of the people. I shall not confine my investigation to the faults of Oregon, though. You know I sometimes write pleasant things as well as unpleasant ones."

Asks About Oregon City.

Then Mr. Steffens turned inquisitor and inquired about Oregon City and its government.

"Have you got any graft?" he asked, and it had to be admitted that we had not.

"Have you got a boss?" was the next question, and again it had to be answered that we were without one since the direct primary law went into operation.

Then he ask about the spirit of the city, whether the citizens were wide awake and progressive, and about the county and its resources, showing his interest in all that concerned Oregon, good or bad.

Mr. Steffens took dinner last night with Mr. U'Ren and left in the evening for Portland. He will remain in the state for some time studying conditions.

Source: Oregon City Enterprise—15 MARCH 1907 [75]

Two articles in the Wednesday, 20 MARCH 1907 edition of *The Morning Oregonian* mentioned Steffens: the first one reported that he had been the guest at the third-annual dinner of the Portland Adman's League held at the Commercial Club the night before; the second one, by Arthur A. Greene, follows:

A CLOSE VIEW OF LINCOLN STEFFENS
MILD-MANNERED BOGIE-MAN WHO TERRIFIES THE GRAFTERS

One of the mildest-mannered bogie-men who ever frightened a year's growth out of a timid little political boss or captain of industry is Lincoln J. Steffens, with whom I had a rendezvous near the fearsome hour of midnight recently in the deserted lobby of the Portland Hotel.

I had kept half a dozen bellboys on the hop all the night through, taking cards to his room, only to discover when at last he did return that he had been in Oregon City talking initiative and referendum with W. S. U'Ren. They must have had a grand little tete-a-tete during the eight hours they visited together.

Mr. Steffens is a smallish man but sturdy, in general appearance suggesting Fred Funston as he looked at the beginning of the Spanish War.[4] He wears a brown Vandyke beard and has

---

[4]Frederick Funston (1865–1917) was a general in the United States Army, known for his service in the Spanish–American War and the Philippine–American War—Ed.

a bookish look, but well as he knows his books he knows men better and is an eminently practical student of his brethren.

I was prepared to find him full of vainglory and dogmatism, as many of our reform writers are, but discovered within a minute after we had shaken hands that he is one of the most companionable men I have ever met. His manner is entirely unaffected, his voice is that particular even baritone that belongs to men with reserve power, and his smile drives away dull care. I imagine he smiles when he is jabbing his harpoon into the corruptionists the hardest, not for the ghoulish pleasure of seeing them squirm, but as an earnest to them that there is no animus back of his efforts. He is not a prosecutor of individuals and it isn't the man he is after—it is the ancient and more or less honorable institution of graft, call it by any other name you will.

I for one am convinced of Steffens' sincerity and I defy any unbiased man to talk to him for half an hour and come to any other conclusion. His work isn't a pleasant one. He could make just as much money writing other things, and he has enough of this world's goods to be in different to Grub street and its venality. He is really convinced that he is discharging a great duty in exposing official and corporation iniquity.

"I'm not much interested in individual wrongdoing," he remarked in a casual way after the disreputable little briar pipe he smokes had begun to warm up.

"If you were to tell me that your City Treasurer had just absconded with $1,000,000 I shouldn't consider that it was a matter that came within my province. But if you were to tell me that a syndicate of bankers had looted Portland of $1,000,000 under the protection of a system of iniquitous laws, then I should immediately proceed to 'get busy'."

"It is less significant to me that some political and business leaders in Oregon stole thousands of acres of the public domain than it is that for years the state virtually indorsed their wrongdoing and became accessory before the fact by continuing them in office and supinely permitting them to have their own way."

"It is a much more important fact that the state has reformed its political methods and made a return to such conditions impossible then that some men were tried and convicted of land frauds."

In spite of his protestation that he isn't interested so much in persons, Mr. Steffens seems curious concerning certain men and ask various questions that might or might not have made them uneasy.

"I shall probably write an article on the land frauds.[5] Of course, that's an old story here, but I'm not writing for Oregon alone. The entire country is interested and is not so familiar with the history of the frauds as you are. My article may not be very timely from a news standpoint, for it will probably not be published for months, but news isn't the essence in such an instance."

"The whole country is also greatly interested in Oregon because she leads the union in the matter of popular government."

Lincoln Steffens.
(c. 1914) [4]

"I've just met and talked with W. S. U'Ren, who, I understand, deserves more credit for bringing about the new order than any other man."

"I've seen all sorts of reformers, but he's a new one to me. I

[5]Steffens published two articles on land frauds: one in SEPTEMBER 1907 called *"The Taming of the West: Discovery of the Land Fraud System; A Detective Story,"* and the second in OCTOBER 1907 called *"The Taming of the West: Heney Grapples the Oregon Land Graft"* [101] [102]—Ed.

have never met a man like him. If the country generally knew of him and his work he would be a conspicuous National figure, and he is likely to become such. Much of the success of your direct election of Senators will depend on the official conduct and ability of Senator Bourne, whom I haven't met. Certainly he has a great opportunity and a greater responsibility. It is 'up to him' to, in a large measure, demonstrate the advantage that will accrue to the whole people through the election of Senators by popular vote rather than by the votes of special interests. The people of all sections are watching him, for they are preparing to follow Oregon's lead and try the experiment for themselves."

The pioneer muck-raker bit at the stem of his pipe when I ask him to name the state that he considered the most corrupt and —shades of Daniel Webster and George F. Hoar! which one do you think he said? Massachusetts! O tempora! O mores! and then some more, O mores![6]

§   §   §

....I believe that Steffens is a California product, graduating at Berkeley with the class of '89. He then went abroad and studied at Berlin, Heidelberg and Leipsic. Two or three years later he returned to this country and got a job as a reporter on the *New York Evening Post.* It so happened that the Wall-street man of the Post was away when the panic of '93 came along and Steffens got the detail. It was here that he first came in contact with the genus grafter and began in a cursory way to look into the shady methods of the financial soiled dove. This assignment over he "went on police" and discovered more things that were not told about in the Sunday school books nor the daily papers either, for that matter. Some time afterward he became city editor of the Commercial Advertiser, which berth he left to take charge of McClure's Magazine as managing editor. Since 1901 when he commenced his series of remarkable articles treating of graft as he has found it he has held a roving commission to go where he

---

[6]Oh what times! Oh what customs!—Ed.

pleases and do pretty much as he pleases. Last Summer in co-partnership with William Allen White, Ida N. Tarbell and John S. Phillips he bought *The American Magazine* which they have built up wonderfully.

It is an interesting arrangement. This association of a quartet of the brightest writers in the country in the business and editorial direction of a magazine. While Mr. Phillips is editor-in-chief each of the four make a hand, as occasion requires, at running the *American* and all of them contribute regularly to it.

Mr. Steffens articles have been so widely read that their author's name is familiar to the entire reading public. The man himself is, however little known the country over. He has taken so many cracks at haughty heads that the "interests" and their friends would have you believe he was almost everything you can think of excepting a high-minded, scholarly writing gentleman who believes he has a mission to perform and is doing his best to keep faith.

Now that he is in Oregon there is certain to be a lot of guessing, but should Lincoln Steffens say sacrilegious things about some of our basswood gods, our senior wardens and noble grands he will believe what he says. In some quarters he is assuredly going to become unpopular, but he's used to that and doesn't care. He keeps his eyes on the game and forgets the grandstand.

Source: *The Morning Oregonian*—20 MARCH 1907 [28]

Steffens and U'Ren met again on the evening of Wednesday, 20 MARCH. Here's what the *Oregon City Courier* reported on Friday, 22 MARCH:

LINCOLN STEFFENS TALKS ON GRAFT

Lincoln Steffens called around on Wednesday evening. He was with William S. U'Ren, the father of the initiative and referendum, the direct primary law, and other kindred blessings. Mr. Steffens came to Oregon City to interview, not to be interviewed, but consented to say a few words about graft and the muck rake.

Pessimist is the word for him, always looking on the dark side of the river, searching for a hidden motive in the goodness of man. He even half believed that Mr. U'Ren was inspired by some ulterior motive, other than patriotism and love for his state, in securing the enactment of laws that allowed Jonathan Bourne to spend a few dollars in order that he might go to Washington as United States senator from Oregon.

"He's a very quiet man," said Mr. Steffens, speaking of U'Ren. He had evidently expected to see a wild-eyed man with a long beard, instead of the mild-mannered man that our distinguished fellow townsmen is.

"What's his game?" went on the great journalist, "What does he want? Has he asked for nothing?"

Then Mr. Steffens settled down comfortably in his chair, took a long pull at his cigar and talked on graft, that he sees in the clouds and hears in the wind. He even picked on poor little Oregon City, with only enough income to pay the interest on its indebtedness, as a shining mark and wanted to know, if you please, if there any grafters here, but he was assured that the word was impossible in the City by the falls.

Mr. Steffens is quiet and unassuming. He said that he had come to Oregon to write up the story of the land frauds, but he would take a look into the merits and workings of the initiative and referendum while he was here. Then he said good night and went with Mr. U'Ren into the seclusion of the private office of that gentleman, where, he secured, presumably what he was after.[7]

Source: *Oregon City Courier*—22 MARCH 1907 [70]

When Steffens was done with his work in Oregon, he went south to California. The *San Francisco Call* reported on 11 APRIL 1907 that he was in San Francisco and staying at the Hotel Imperial [96].

Lincoln Steffens published his portrait of U'Ren a year later. It follows next in Chapter 4.

[7]The law firm of *U'Ren and Schuebel* had their office in the Enterprise Building in downtown Oregon City at the intersection of 6th and Main Street. The interview likely took place there. The Enterprise Building is shown above on a 1900 Sanborn-Perris fire insurance map—Ed.

4

U'REN, THE LAWGIVER

LINCOLN STEFFENS' PORTRAIT OF William S. U'Ren, published in MARCH 1908 in *The American Magazine*, and then in 1909 as a chapter in Steffens' book *Upbuilders*, made U'Ren a nationally known figure. Almost every newspaper story, magazine article, history book, academic paper, and web-site post written about U'Ren in the last 100 years, has relied on Steffens' *U'Ren, The Law-giver*.

Some modern readers may struggle with some of Steffens' prose and expressions. As this will be the third retelling of the Initiative and Referendum story in this work, you have permission to move on to the next chapter.

If you want to learn more about U'Ren the man, you will be rewarded by Steffens' presentation.

Steffens does get some facts wrong, such as when U'Ren first learned about the Single Tax; your humble editor has added footnotes, where needed, to set the record straight on those points.

At the end of the story, Steffens touches on U'Ren's political activities after the Initiative and Referendum were added to the Oregon Constitution. Chapter 5 explains how U'Ren went on to use the 'tools' he had helped to install to create what became known as the 'Oregon System'.

U'Ren, The Law-giver

The Legislative Blacksmith of Oregon and the Tools He's Fashioned for Democracy

By Lincoln Steffens

Oregon has more fundamental legislation than any other state in the Union excepting only Oklahoma, and Oklahoma is new. Oregon is not new; it is and it long has been corrupt, yet it has enacted laws which enable its people to govern themselves when they want to. How did this happen? How did this state of graft get all her tools for democracy? And, since it has them, why don't her people use them more? The answer to these questions lies buried deep in the character and in the story of W. S. U'Ren (accent the last syllable), the lawgiver.

They call this man the Father of the Initiative and Referendum in Oregon, but that title isn't big enough. U'Ren has fathered other Oregon laws, and his own state isn't the limit of his influence. The Dakotas have some similar legislation. Meeting on a Western train one day a politician who seemed to know all about things there, I inquired into the origin of the Dakota laws.

William S. U'Ren
(c. 1908) [103]

"There's a fellow over in Oregon," he answered—"funny name—he tipped us off and steered us; sent drafts of bills and pamphlets containing arguments. I can't recall his name."

"U'Ren?"

"That's it; that's the man."

They are getting good laws in the State of Washington, also. I asked in Seattle where they came from. Very few knew, but those that did said: "U'Ren of Oregon."

The first time I heard this name was in Rhode Island. Ex-Governor Garvin, the advocate of democratic legislation for that law-bound state, knew about U'Ren.[1] After that I used to come upon his influence in many states and cities where men were tinkering with the sacred constitutional machinery that won't let democracy go. But my last encounter with the mysterious ubiquity of this singular man's influence was amusing. Spreckels, Heney, and the other fighters for San Francisco thought of going to the people on a certain proposition and, seeing thus the uses of the referendum, wanted it. I suggested writing to U'Ren. They never had heard of him, but they wrote, and he came. And he heard them out on their need of the referendum.

"But I think," said U'Ren, "that you have it in your city charter." Everybody looked incredulous. "Where is the book?" U'Ren asked. "I think I can find it. I certainly had some correspondence with the makers of that charter; I think I drafted a section—yes, here it is. [He read it to himself.] It isn't mine—not very clear—but [handing back the book] good enough for your purpose, you see."

William Simon U'Ren, the lawgiver, was born JANUARY 10, 1859, at Lancaster, Wisconsin. His father is a blacksmith, and his father's seven brothers were blacksmiths; their father was a blacksmith, and their father's father, and his father, and his.[2] As far as the family can trace from Cornwall, England, back into Holland, they see an unbroken line of blacksmiths. And preachers.

[1] Lucius Fayette Clark Garvin (1841–1922). As governor of Rhode Island he supported the extension of suffrage to foreign-born citizens, advocated for proportional representation, and supported, as did U'Ren, the single tax economic theory of Henry George—Ed.

[2] U'Ren father was more than just a blacksmith during his life. See Chapters 7, 8, and 9—Ed.

Five of U'Ren's seven uncles preached and, among their ancestors, other blacksmiths preached. And William U'Ren himself
is both a blacksmith and a preacher in a way; in a very essential
way.

"Blacksmithing is my trade," he says. "And it has always given
colour to my view of things. For example, when I was very
young, I saw some of the evils in the conditions of life, and I
wanted to fix them. I couldn't. There were no tools. We had
tools to do almost anything with in the shop, beautiful tools,
wonderful. And so in other trades, arts and professions; in everything but government. In government, the common trade of
all men and the basis of all social life, men worked still with old
tools, with old laws, with constitutions and charters which hin-
dered more than they helped. Men suffered from this. There
were lawyers enough; many of our ablest men were lawyers.
Why didn't some of them invent legislative implements to help
the people govern themselves? Why had we no tool makers for
democracy?"

U'Ren is a very quiet man. He never would strike one as a
blacksmith. He never would strike one at all. Slight of figure,
silent in motion, he speaks softly, evenly, as he walks; and they
call him, therefore, the "pussy cat."

"You see," he purred now, "I saw it all in terms of the mechanic."

But he feels it all in the terms of religion. His mother, also Cornish, also of the class that labours hard, was also religious—a
Methodist. She taught her children from the Bible. Jehovah,
Moses, and Jesus were the ideals of this humble family, and,
for some reason, Moses caught the imagination of her oldest
boy, William. He always wanted to hear about Moses, the law-
giver, and when he could read for himself, Exodus and Num-
bers were the books he loved best. And just as some boys want
to be Napoleon, so young U'Ren dreamed that when he grew
up he would be like Moses, the giver of laws that should lead
the people out of Darkness into the land of Promise. But, of
course, the Biblical hero-worship, taught him first by that pious

woman, his good mother, made it a religious influence, as it still is, for when U'Ren, the blacksmith, is fashioning his legislative tools he works not alone with the affection of the true mechanic, but with the devotion of faith that his laws will indeed deliver the people from bondage.

All his life William U'Ren had heard of liberty. His father's father lived in Cornwall on land leased for ninety-nine years; his mother's father on land leased for "three lives." That's why his father emigrated at seventeen, and his mother at ten, to the "land of the free." And one of William's first recollections of "American liberty" is of our war against slavery. His mother told stories of "poor little black children sold away from their mothers," and his father pointed out the power of the "slave interest." He realized the Power of Evil, that father did.

A strong, independent spirit, he wanted to work for himself. He was an expert mechanic. The son tells how once when they got a job together, he boasted of his father's skill, and the next time a piece of work came along calling for a master workman, the elder U'Ren was put to it. He did it to a turn "in one heat." So he was in demand as "a hand," but he had a head and he "hated a boss." He wouldn't stick to a good job, no matter how good it was. He must "move on," seeking liberty—freedom to do his own work in his own way. He couldn't. The best pay for a blacksmith was in big organizations like the copper mines of Lake Superior. He tried farming. He led his family West, from Wisconsin to Nebraska; over into Colorado; back to Wisconsin; down again to Wyoming and Colorado. It was no use. Father and sons, they all worked as only border farmers work; they couldn't earn enough ahead to buy their liberty; or, if they got a start, something set them back.

U'Ren visualized one tragic day out of this life for me. His father had taken up a homestead in Nebraska, and they had made a farm of it. William remembers halting, on his way to town one morning, to look back from a hill over the rich, yellow level of their crops spread out under the sun. When he came home that afternoon, he stopped, stunned, on that same hill-top. The sun still shone, but the homestead, the whole country, was bare and brown. The boy understood then what one of the plagues of Egypt was. The grasshoppers had passed, a cyclone of them, and in four hours the U'Rens were ruined.

"I was brought up in the fear of the poor," U'Ren says, "the terrible fear of poverty." But not in hate; at least, not in the hatred of men. "Things make men do bad things," he says. He does not believe in bad men and good men, and, as we shall see, he deals placidly with both kinds. "Conditions are to blame for all evil," he pleads patiently, "conditions that can be changed." His father, who pointed out conditions to him, taught him also to fight. But he was to fight for justice, not for hate.

Since the family moved about so much, William seemed always to be "the new boy" at school. The others picked on him. He was still a child, quick-tempered, but not aggressive. And the first time he was tempted to fight, when he was seven years old, he took his mother's counsel that only

> "Dogs delight to bark and bite;
> It is their nature to."

William didn't fight. But when, not long after that, at Neva-daville, Colorado, Davie Radcliffe called Willie U'Ren a liar, Willie consulted his father. The father reflected a moment, then said in a way the boy never forgot:

"Never hunt a fight, boy, but never run from one; never suffer wrong or injustice."

The next day Willie U'Ren hunted the fight he had avoided. He found Davie; Davie didn't care to fight then. But another boy accommodated Willie. Johnnie Badger, the fighter of the school, licked Willie that day; and the next; and the next. Willie came back for his licking till his father happened to hear of it.

"What's the matter, William?" he asked. "Can't you lick that boy?"

"Not yet," said William, "but I will some day."

The father took his boy in hand, taught him how to use his fists and—Willie went to school and licked Johnnie Badger. "And then," U'Ren says, "we became good friends."

A salient trait of U'Ren, the man, is his perfect self-possession. His father developed that in him. One day William was sent to a neighbour's for a set of double-trees for a wagon. He hitched a trace to it and, letting his horse drag it home, lost one of the clevis pins. His father rebuked him sharply, and William flew into one of his violent but infrequent passions. His father was silent. He didn't want to break the boy's spirit; he waited till William "felt bad." They were haying together then, and at one of the pauses to rest the father talked quietly about self-control. One must learn to govern one's self, he said, and he concluded: "If *you* don't, William, *you* might *kill*."

No one who meets W. S. U'Ren now could believe that he ever had a temper. It took time, but the character-building done for the boy both by his parents and by himself was good work well done. And his mental development was still more interesting. Though his father's discontent kept the conditions of their life critically before him, there was no understanding of causes. They read "Greeley's Paper," [3] and both father and son followed politics. But the first definite sense of the economic problems underlying politics came to William himself when he was hardly thirteen. The farmers in the Nebraska district where his father had his homestead, needing a school, met to devise ways of making the absentee land-owners pay for it.

"It seemed to me, as a boy," U'Ren now, "that something was wrong in this. If it was right for those non-voting landholders to own the land, it was wrong to tax them for the school they did not use. Or, if it was right to tax them, it was wrong for them to

[3] The *New York Tribune*, published by Horace Greeley (1811–1872), was widely read west of the Mississippi. Greeley was a Progressive Republican, an abolitionist, and a strong prohibitionist—Ed.

hold the land they did not use. I puzzled over this, but I could not put my finger on the injustice I felt lurking somewhere."

He never spoke of this. He was a solitary soul, as his sports show. He didn't dance, nor even play much. He liked to hunt and think, to work and think, to read and—dream. While he learned his trade, and learned to love and while he worked the farm and took pride in his rows of corn, his ambition ran off to politics. But not to the game. Congress was his goal. That was where the lawgivers gathered. To fit himself to make laws, he must study law and, in Denver, he entered an office as student,[4] but not with the idea of making law his career. One of the firm, Merrick A. Rogers,[5] encouraged U'Ren there. "Money-getting isn't a very high object, not for life," he used to say. And despite his terror of poverty, U'Ren has always regarded the practice of his profession as secondary consideration. He is a legislator.

Politics comes first with U'Ren. He makes his living with his left hand; his right for the state. And that such citizenship can be effective demonstrated by this remarkable fact: The Father of the Initiative and Referendum, the first legislator of Oregon, has held office but once in his career. He has done what he has done as a citizen in politics.

His first experience of the game was in Denver when he was a law student. The Presidential campaign of 1880 was on and U'Ren had just come of age. The Republican party needed the help of all good men and true, and first-voters were invited to work. U'Ren volunteered.

He offered his services with the enthusiasm of youth and the fervour of that secret inspiration of Moses. And the leaders welcomed the boy. They put him to work. They directed him to aid in colonizing voters in a doubtful ward!

[4]France & Rogers—Ed.

[5]Judge Merrick Austin Rogers (1838–1901) would later shock and horrify the citizens of Steamboat Springs, Colorado, when he committed suicide with a stick of blasting powder—Ed.

U'Ren was stunned. He did not know such things were done.[6] He was horrified, but fascinated. He said nothing; he didn't do the work, but he hung about watching it done. The dreamer was allowed to see the inside. There were anti-Chinese riots in the town. The mob marched through the streets crying "The Chinese must go!" and threatening to kill them. U'Ren became excited. Here was oppression of the weak. At his request, he was appointed a deputy to "protect the poor Chinamen," and he served in all earnestness till an insider explained to him that the mob was organized and the riots were faked—to get the good citizens out to the polls to vote for "law and order and the party."[7]

The elders forget how young people feel when first discover that the world isn't what schools and grown-ups have taught them. It would be better to teach the truth; then the new citizens would be prepared for the fray. As it is, the sudden shock carries away not only the "illusions," but more often the character of youth. Not so with U'Ren, however. His dream of Congress vanished, but his hope of inventing laws to make such evils less easy and profitable—that stayed. Indeed, this was the time when the dominant idea of his life took its first definite form.

"As I watched this fraud, and saw that it was the means by which the other evils were maintained, I felt clearly that a modicum of the thought and ingenuity which had been devoted to machinery, if given to government, would make this a pleasant world to live in. That men were all right at bottom, I was convinced, for I noticed that we young men were honest and capable of some unselfish service. It was the older men that were 'bad.' "

[6] 'Colonizing voters' was the fraudulent practice of buying purchasable electors and moving them into a district before the time of voting—Ed.

[7] On Sunday, 31 OCTOBER 1880, two days before the election, a mob of 3,000 Democratic Party supporters gathered in Denver's Chinatown outside a saloon where a Chinese man had been attacked. A speech by the Mayor and the arrival of Denver's 30-man police force did not pacify the mob. Over the next ten hours, the rioters destroyed Chinese homes and businesses, and attacked and beat Chinese people, killing one man [126]—Ed.

Sickness befell U'Ren, a long, lingering, weakening illness, that took all the sand out of him. He was admitted to the bar, and practised long enough to see the trickery and the injustice of the Law.[8] He edited a newspaper at Tin Cup, a mining town, but he saw that that business had its frauds, too, and that the editor is no freer than his father, the blacksmith, was. So he quit, and began just such a wandering life as his father had led. In pursuit of liberty and health, he moved about from Denver to Iowa, back to Colorado, on to California, the Hawaiian Islands, and Oregon, and back, getting better and worse till 1889–90, when something happened; something for which these wander-years and his whole life and his father's had prepared him.

He read "Progress and Poverty."[9] It is wonderful how many of the men who are working for political reform got their inspiration from Henry George. "I am for men," George said, and he made men. No matter what the world may decide to do about his single tax, some day it will have to acknowledge that Henry George brought into the service of man more men of more different kinds than any other man of his day. U'Ren is not an orthodox single-taxer to-day; U'Ren cannot be classified economically at all; he thinks for himself. He read other books then; he reads other books now. Open-minded in the period when, as he says, "the hard conditions and selfish interests of life are ossifying most men," he never has been able to close up his mind. He is wide open to any truth from any source.

The way he started on his career as a legislator shows this. One day toward the end of his wander-years, as he was changing from the train to the boat on the Oakland (California) mole, somebody thrust into his hand a leaflet on the "initiative." There was nothing about the "referendum," and U'Ren had never heard of either. But he had noticed that all the political evils

[8]U'Ren was admitted to the Colorado bar on 31 JANUARY 1881. He practiced law in Colorado for six years, from 1881 to 1887. See Chapter 7 for more details—Ed.

[9]U'Ren read *Progress and Poverty* in 1882; see Appendix B—Ed.

of all the cities and states, where he had idly watched men defeat themselves, culminated in the betrayal of the people by their representatives. And this leaflet showed how the people themselves, outside of and over the heads of their elected representatives, might initiate and pass laws. Here was a tool for democracy; here was a means to achieve the reforms Henry indicated. U'Ren determined then and there to hammer this leaflet into a bill and pass it—somewhere.

U'Ren didn't care where. The need of it was universal in the United States. He thought how useful it would be in Denver, in Iowa, in Wisconsin; it was needed right there in California. But he happened to be going to Oregon and—that's how U'Ren came to be the lawgiver "of Oregon."[10]

The initiative—as a tool, remember; as a means to an end; as a first political step toward changing our economic conditions—this idea gave purpose to his life. His health improved. He went to Portland and, mousing around for books and men, came upon E. W. Bingham.[11]

"Ed. Bingham," U'Ren says, "was a lawmaker. He had the most wonderful constructive talent for law-building that I ever encountered."

Bingham was working with an Australian Ballot League.[12] He was secretary, and he taught U'Ren to be secretary of things. "Never be president," he said. "Never be conspicuous. Get a president and a committee; and let them go to the front. The worker must work behind them, out of sight. Be secretary."

[10] U'Ren's father, mother, and siblings had settled in Oregon in 1881—Ed.

[11] Edward Wingard Bingham (1851–1904) was a railroad confidential agent, well-known lawyer, ardent sportsman and hunter, and inventor, with patents (including NO. 372,652 issued on 8 NOVEMBER 1887 on a 'sectional horseshoe') promoted by Bingham and his brother John in a failed joint-venture called the "Bingham Sectional Horseshoe Co." based in Bridgeport, Connecticut—Ed.

[12] The full story of Bingham's campaign to have Oregon enact the Australian Ballot system can be found in Appendix A—Ed.

U'Ren has always been secretary; clerical, impersonal, but busy, like Bingham. He has given credit for all his work to other men. The first time I met him, he talked of leagues and committees of leading citizens—bankers, railroad men, corporation attorneys, corrupt politicians—whom he named. But I noticed that while the members of U'Ren's several committees knew something about their own work, they seldom knew anything about that of the other committees of which U'Ren was secretary; and when it came to precise information, they all would say, "You must see our secretary, a Mr. U'Ren, for that." A Mr. U'Ren was the one man in Oregon who knew all about all this legislation.

Well, Bingham had drawn the Australian ballot law for his league, and he talked it over, section by section, with U'Ren, who thus got from an expert his first lesson in law-building. The next thing was to pass it. U'Ren asked why they didn't get the platform committee of the Republican Convention to endorse the bill. Bingham laughed, and so did a senator who was present, but the dreamer "rushed in where angels feared to tread." You will hear to-day in Oregon that U'Ren is "the smoothest lobbyist" in the state, and he is. He is calm, conciliating, persistent; and he fits his argument to his man. He talked politics to that platform committee; he gave, not his reasons for wanting the Australian ballot, but arguments which appealed to these party politicians. And they listened. Then Bingham appeared. Unlike U'Ren, Bingham was aggressive. He came into the committee room with fire in his eye, bulldozing, begging, reasoning, and threatening. They could put off U'Ren; Bingham hung on like a bulldog, and in the end, they got his bill endorsed by the Republicans. Then they went to the Democratic Convention and there also they won. And the Legislature, thus pledged, adopted Bingham's Australian ballot.

Started thus first in the public service, U'Ren had still to make his living. About that time he fell in with an interesting group of people, the Luellings of Milwaukie (Oregon), orchardists and nurserymen.[13] Seth developed the well-known cherries, "Bing" and the "Black Republican" which latter the South re-named the "Luelling." Seth and his wife, and Alfred Luelling, were live-minded people, and they gathered about them other active brains. They thought, and they read; they had lectures and they recited from the English poets. Lacking orthodox teachers, they guided themselves through studies from economics to spiritualism. Unafraid of any new idea, they gave a welcome and a hearing to any apostle of any ism. U'Ren was well received among them. He was taken into partnership in the business. When that failed in the panic of 1893, there was a quarrel, and bitter feelings which endure to this day, but U'Ren says that his health, his heart, and his mind all were better for this life among these people.

It was here that he heard first of the referendum. They were all members of the Farmers' Alliance, and Alfred Luelling brought to a meeting one night J. W. Sullivan's book on direct legislation in Switzerland. It contained the whole set of tools of which, hitherto, U'Ren had heard of but one, the initiative. This would enable the people to make laws; the referendum would enable them to stop legislation initiated by their legislators. U'Ren was enthusiastic; the whole alliance was. With these tools, the people could really govern themselves. And that is what these people wanted; they were Populists.

We of the East despised the "Pops"; but their movement was to the reform movement of today what the "extreme" Abolitionists of New England were to the great movement that produced Lincoln and the Republican party. U'Ren became a Populist. But that party was to him—what the Republican party is to him now; what any party must be to any man who has in mind the good, not of an organization, but of a people—a means to an end, an instrument, a political tool. The "Pops" were sincere people who wanted to change things for the better. There was

[13]The family name was spelled two ways by its members: 'Luelling' and 'Lewelling'—Ed.

a use for them, and U'Ren, who saw it, joined them and soon was secretary of the Populist State Committee.

And when, as secretary of the Populists, he had worked the initiative and referendum plank into their platform, he went forth as secretary of a Direct Legislation League to the conventions of the other parties. And he lobbied initiative and referendum planks into the platforms of all of them, excepting only the Prohibitionists, who, like the Socialists, "won't play" with anybody else. Having the parties pledged, he set about making them keep their promises. He lighted a fire behind them.

U'Ren went to the people. They were ready for him. The year was 1893. Discontent was widespread. Agitation had taken the form of a demand that the Legislature to be elected in 1894 should call a constitutional convention to rectify all evils, and U'Ren was one of the many workers who went about pledging candidates. But he and the Luellings concentrated on the "I. & R.," as they called the initiative and referendum. As secretary of the Direct Legislation League he got up a folder stating simply the democratic principle underlying the initiative and referendum and the results to be expected from it. Direct legislation was an acknowledgment of the right of the people to govern themselves and a device to enable them to do so. The "I. & R." would put it in the power of the voters to start or stop any legislation, just like a boss. In other words, it would make the people boss; the legislators would have to represent the voters who elected them, not railroads and not any other "interest." Nobody could object (openly) to this; at least, nobody would out there in that Western state where the failures of democracy were ascribed, not as in the East, to the people, but to the business and political interests that actually are to blame.

Everybody worked. The women sewed the folders; two-thirds of the houses in Milwaukie were thus engaged that winter (1893–94); they prepared 50,000 folders in English and 18,000 in German; and the alliances and labour unions saw that the voters got and read them. The effect was such that when the politicians pleaded ignorance of the initiative and referendum, U'Ren could answer: "The people know about them." And that was, true. After the election, these same workers, men and women, circulated a petition which, with 14,000 signatures, was presented to the Legislature.

Now, that is as far as a reform movement usually goes. U'Ren went further. Knowing that the representatives elected by the people are organized in the Legislature to represent somebody else, U'Ren went to Salem as a lobbyist, a lobbyist for the people, and he talked to every member of that Legislature. He saw the chicanery, fraud, and the politics of it all, but he wrung from a clear majority promises to keep their pledge.

"And we lost," he told me quietly. "We lost by one vote in the House and in the Senate also—by one vote."

"Fooled?" I asked.

"Fooled," said U'Ren. "It was done in the Senate by a wink, a wink from Joe Simon" (president of the Senate and boss of Portland).

"You understood. How did you feel?"

"We were angry," U'Ren answered. "I completely lost my self-control and I said and did things that were wrong. And when I saw my mistake, I remembered what my father used to say about self-control, and I tied a string on my finger to remind me. That device of the children worked with me. I think I never afterward completely lost my temper."

The act which U'Ren calls his mistake was to go out from that Legislature to punish the members who had broken their pledges; and that is what I can't help believing must be done. But U'Ren is one of those very, very few men that believe, after these 2,000 years, in the Christian spirit as a *practical* force.

"Alfred Luelling first questioned the wisdom," he said, "of punishing faithless legislators. We talked it over and I thought a lot about it. And I decided that he was right. After that, we never punished men. Of course, we voted against a delinquent, if the parties gave us a choice; but our policy was to publish, not a man's delinquencies, but his promises."

Coming from a practical politician, this is a most important tip for reformers. And U'Ren is a practical politician. He learned from that Legislature. Watching it as, when a boy, he watched Denver politics, open-eyed, he saw what he saw, and his mind, never taught to blink the facts, took in what his ears and eyes perceived. When he came home, he organized his county, and he organized it well. The "dreamer" became the boss of his (Clackamas) county, but he was not a selfish boss. This was his chance to realize his young dream of Congress. The Populists wanted him to go, but he knew now what Congress was, and "What could I have done against the combine that ran it?" he asked. "I could do nothing but protest at Washington," he added. "In Oregon I could get the initiative and referendum through."

So he ran for the assembly and was elected. This was in 1896. Bryan was running for President, and Oregon was a Free Silver state. Even Republicans like Senator Mitchell were for silver; they were called "Silver Republicans" just as in the East we had "Gold Democrats." The Populists elected thirteen assemblymen, the Democrats three, the Republicans forty-four; in the senate the Populists had three votes, the Democrats three, the Republicans twenty-four. And this is important because that Legislature never was organized; it was the famous hold-up session, a scandal yet in Oregon. And U'Ren was one of the managers of that hold-up. Oh, he had learned a lot of politics!

The demand for a constitutional convention was waning. Leaders like U'Ren realized that a convention might amenable to public opinion as the Legislature, so he was for the initiative and referendum by legislative amendment. That would require the passage of the resolution through two legislatures in succession and then a vote by the people. This way looked long, but U'Ren, as a boy, had proven on Johnnie Badger that he was built to fight till he won. And he had a plan. He had seen in the last session how a delegation such as the "Pops" had now could be used to play politics with, and U'Ren had made up his mind to play politics—for the people. He began right after election.

Oregon at the time was in that primitive stage of corruption where personalities still played a part and any cash briber had a chance for high office. The railroads ruled, but the dominant road, the Southern Pacific, was a foreign corporation. Its bosses might have gone to the United States Senate from Oregon if they had lived there, but they were elected by California, so Oregon was open to its own rich men. And many of them sought the "honour." They paid out great sums trying to get it. The politicians told me that these bankers, editors and business men were "played for suckers" year after year; and any Oregonian will tell you with a laugh the names of the victims of this long-drawn-out comedy.

U'Ren understood this. In 1897 Senator Mitchell was to be re-elected; U'Ren had no doubt of that, and he called on him to trade "Pop" votes for his help on the initiative and referendum. Politician as he was, Mitchell talked favourably in August, not at all in November, and just before the session, "went back on" the measure entirely. He told U'Ren why.

"I've got three "Pop" votes that nobody can get away," he said.

"Are you sure?" asked U'Ren, who could hardly believe that the Populists, so new and so enthusiastic, would surrender so soon to "the conditions that make men bad."

Mitchell was sure; he advised U'Ren not to introduce the bill. "My people won't stand for it," the Senator said.

Mitchell had made one other shift of position. A Silver Republican all through the Oregon campaign (which ended in the June election), he came out after it for McKinley and gold. Some of his lieutenants left him, among them Jonathan Bourne, Jr., a man we must know. He is now a United States Senator from Oregon. You have heard of black sheep? Well, Bourne was the black ram of a rich old New England family. After a wild time at Harvard University and a wilder time "about town," he went West and had the wildest time of all. I think U'Ren will not charge him up to conditions; I've heard him say that Bourne was improved by age. Bourne learned his game from Mitchell, who learned his from Quay in Pennsylvania, whence Mitchell came (after a change of name). And the lesson of the Quay school of politics was not to organize like Tammany for the year around, but to "let her rip" till just before a campaign, then make a new "combine."

When Mitchell made his gold "combine," Bourne made his new silver "combine" and—U'Ren joined Bourne. Mitchell didn't have the three Pop votes. U'Ren found that his delegation was solid, and ready to trade. All they wanted was (1) the initiative and referendum, (2) a good registration law (Ed. Bingham's), and (3) Pop judges and clerks of elections. Bourne wanted to be Speaker. He was willing to swing his delegation to the Pop bills in return for their votes for his speakership. This settled the House; they looked to the Senate. The President, Joe Simon, was the man who beat the constitutional convention with a wink. No matter. U'Ren wasn't punishing men. He called on Simon. He knew Simon wanted to go to the United States Senate. Simon didn't say so. No. Simon's conversation suggested that President Corbett of the First National Bank would make a good Senator, but the politicians understood that Corbett was "only Simon's rich sucker." And so it turned out, for when, later, Simon did control a legislature for Corbett, Simon, not Corbett, was elected to the United States Senate. But U'Ren wasn't interested in senatorships. He believed that Simon would go into a strong combine to beat Mitchell. And he was right. Since the terms—U'Ren's "fool" legislation and Bourne's speakership—were satisfactory, Simon delivered the Senate.

Does it begin to appear now how U'Ren got his good laws in the bad state of Oregon? Do you begin to understand why it was that "leading citizens" and "corrupt politicians," the very men who are against reform elsewhere, "passed all these reform measures ascribed to U'Ren?" Most of these men didn't know what they were doing, and they didn't care. They wanted something for themselves; U'Ren wanted something for the people. On that basis, William U'Ren went into every political deal that he could get into.

And that he was a factor to be reckoned with, he proved right away. Quick, quiet, industrious, he had his "combine" organized before Mitchell woke up. The Simon-Bourne-Pop crowd captured the temporary organization of the House. This they did by a snap. They weren't ready to elect a United States Senator, and since the election must be held, by law, on the second Tuesday after the permanent organization was effected, their play was to put off the election of a Speaker. U'Ren himself made that play. There was a contest over one seat in the House. U'Ren was on the committee and he controlled three of the five votes. He wouldn't report. The minority, seeing the game, rushed back and, reporting a row in the committee, caused a row in the House. And a mad scene it was. The Mitchell men rose in a rage and, all on their feet, were crying "Fraud!" and demanding "Action." When U'Ren arrived, his side, uninformed and without a leader, was in a state of confusion. They greeted him with a cheer and he took the floor. Quietly, with great courtesy and unexpected ability, he met the attack. Everybody else was excited. U'Ren alone was cool and, as man after man arose to accuse him, he, with the papers they wanted in his pocket, answered with reason and with tact. And his self-possession soon possessed the House. "It is wonderful!" a woman spectator exclaimed. "Whenever that man speaks, you can feel a sense of quiet settle upon the whole House." Little known in the state and known to the politicians as "the dreamer," U'Ren's debate that night made him a reputation. The recollection of everybody present was vivid ten years afterward, when I inquired, but when I mentioned it to U'Ren, he smiled; he never fools himself.

"It is easy to make a reputation as a parliamentarian," he said, "when you have the chairman on your side."

He won out; that is what he recalls. He beat permanent organization that Monday night, and thus put off the senatorial vote for two weeks. And then followed, not two weeks, but a session, of bribery, drunkenness, hate, and deadlock. Men were bought, sold, and bought back again. Both sides used money fiercely; and since there was no appropriation bill, the members got from the state no salary, no mileage, nothing; they had to have money. Well, they got it. Bourne set up a private house, somewhat like the "House of Mirth" at Albany, N.Y., where he "kept" men on his side. Mitchell ran the price of votes up to thousands of dollars, and he and his lieutenant, Charlie Fulton (later a United States Senator from Oregon), paid out the money in cash. The Pops caught them at it.

Johnson Smith, assistant warden of the Penitentiary, then a Pop assemblyman, proposed to go to Mitchell and take some of his money for evidence.

"Go ahead," said U'Ren. "We'll vouch for your purpose in doing it."

So Smith got from Mitchell and Fulton $1,500 as for himself, and $250 as for the go-between. The next day, when the Mitchell men were trying to gather a quorum, Smith stood outside in the lobby. Rushing up to him, Fulton ordered him to his seat. Smith laughed.

"Why! Aren't you going in?" said Fulton. And when Smith said he wasn't, Fulton flew into a rage. "Didn't you take our money and promise to go in?"

"Yes," said Smith, "I took your money. You were so damn fresh and free with it, I thought I'd take a piece. But it's you that's sold, not me."

There was more to this dialogue, but the sequel will interest the people of the United States who want to know about their

United States Senators. Governor (now U. S. Senator) Chamberlain of Oregon made an affidavit for Francis J. Heney to send to President Roosevelt, deposing and swearing that when Smith was under consideration for appointment to the penitentiary, Fulton protested on the ground, not that Smith had taken Mitchell's money, but that, having taken he had not stayed bought! Charles W. Fulton is fundamentally corrupt.

"No," says U'Ren. "That was in war time, and we mustn't judge men in the heat of battle by the standards of cold blood." But U'Ren is excusing the bribery of 1897; the Senator's protest to Governor Chamberlain was in 1903—in cold blood. But never mind Fulton. How about U'Ren? That deadlock, which he helped to manage, lasted to the end. Nothing was accomplished; no Senator was elected, no legislation passed, and everybody concerned was under suspicion. U'Ren himself had charges to answer. He was accused of taking money from Bourne, and calling together the Pop committee, he admitted that he had borrowed $80. He had to, he pleaded. He had opened a law office in Oregon City, but a "country lawyer" in politics earns very little, and since there was no appropriation bill, he got no pay as an assemblyman. He earned none, he admitted, and he abided by that. For when the next Legislature voted full salaries and mileage to its predecessor, U'Ren and one other member, George Ogle, sent back their warrants. So he never did get any money for that time and, to exist, he had to borrow from Bourne. But the $80 was a loan, not a bribe; he has long since paid it back and, since he suggested the whole deal, the money did not affect his conduct. His committee exonerated U'Ren, but the transaction hurt him, and so did some letters of his which, published later, showed how he traded with the powers of evil; as he did and as he went on doing—deliberately, in cold blood, as George Ogle knows.

George Ogle, farmer and Populist, is notoriously honest. He was U'Ren's best friend, and when in the fall of 1898 Ogle's mother died, he asked U'Ren to deliver the funeral address.

The next day Ogle mounted his horse and rode back to town with U'Ren. It was a cold ride in the rain through slush, but they had a warm talk, those two. U'Ren had run for the Senate that summer against George C. Brownell, the Senator from Clackamas who, as chairman on the committee on railroads, had represented for years the corrupt system of Oregon in the Senate. He beat U'Ren, who turned right around and made a deal with him. U'Ren promised to help elect Brownell to any office he might choose to run for next time, if the Senator would work in good faith for the initiative and referendum. Ogle knew this because he was one of the "Pops" U'Ren had asked to join in his bargain. And Ogle had been thinking it over ever since, and now, out there in the mud and sleet of that country road, he asked U'Ren what the fight was to cost him, U'Ren.

U'Ren understood, and he answered, "I am going to get the initiative and referendum in Oregon," he said, "if it costs me my soul. I'll do nothing selfish, dishonest, or dishonourable, but I'll trade off parties, offices, bills—anything for that."

Ogle objected. "Good things are not worth that price," he said.

They were both thinking of Brownell, of course, and U'Ren said he had to deal with the men in office. "We can't choose our human instruments," he argued, "and we can't change political methods till we have passed some legal tools to do it with." And he recalled a story Ogle had told him once of a cattleman who discharged a cowboy because he returned from a search for some cattle with an explanation of his failure to find them. "I want my cattle, not your excuses," the cattleman said, and "that," said U'Ren, "is what the people say to us." It was the old question whether the end justifies the means.

They quarrelled over it, those two good friends. It was a quiet quarrel and it is being made up now, but they parted then for many years, Ogle returning to his farm, U'Ren to the lobby at Salem.

And U'Ren used the lobbyist's means to attain his end. He

and Frank Williams[14] watched their "friends" and made new ones. Brownell was true; also he was clever. He didn't pretend to believe in the "crank" measure. "I've got to vote for it," he would say to his "practical" colleagues. "My district is chock-full of 'Pops' and I have to placate them. And what does the initiative and referendum amount to anyway? It's got to go through two sessions. Pass it now and we can beat it next time." But Brownell's best service was in trading. Once, for example, Williams, one of Lincoln's old secret-service men, learned that two Senators were quarrelling over an appropriation for a normal school. U'Ren arranged through Brownell to get appropriations for both. Two normal schools appropriations for two "I. & R." votes! And it was either at this session or the next that U'Ren and his friends connived at what he calls a "vicious gerrymander."

"We helped through measures we didn't believe in," U'Ren says in his plain way, "to get help for our measures from members who didn't believe in them. That's corruption, yes; that's a kind of corruption, but our measures were to make corruption impossible in the end."

The "I. & R." passed in 1899, 44 to 8 in the House, 22 to 6 in the Senate. And U'Ren went on working. The moment the session closed, the Direct Legislation League (W. S. U'Ren, secretary) set about making it impossible for Brownell's friends to "beat it next time." U'Ren instructed the voters. The propaganda was systematic, thorough, complete, and the politicians knew it. And the politicians knew now that U'Ren's word was good, and his support worth having. So in 1901, when the measure came up for second passage, U'Ren, from the lobby and after more dickering, saw it go through unanimously. And at

---

[14]Born in New York, Frank Williams (1839–1911) became a wealthy, self-made man in Kansas before coming to Oregon in 1890, where he met U'Ren and they became closely associated in political matters. U'Ren considered Williams' work for the Initiative and Referendum indispensable—Ed.

the next general election (1902) the people approved 11 to 1.

Thus it was, then, that the people of Oregon achieved actual sovereignty over their corrupted state—by the methods of corruption. What good has it done them? They have the power to change their constitution at will; to make laws and to veto acts of their Legislature, but laws and machinery are of no use to people unless there are leaders to apply them. The referendum which U'Ren found in the charter of San Francisco was a dead letter; Heney didn't even know it was there. And Heney's exposure of Oregon came two years after U'Ren had his "I. & R." In brief, to repeat the question raised at the beginning of our story, Why don't the people of Oregon use their power to change the system?

The answer as before, "W. U'Ren." He knows the "I. & R." is nothing but a tool; that it is worth while only as can be used to change the "conditions that make men do bad things"; and he means to use it. Indeed, he proposed, when he got it, to proceed at once to economic reforms. But wiser heads counselled that, until the new instrument had been tempered by custom, would be better to use the "I. & R." only to get other new tools. So the Direct Legislation League gave way to Direct Primary League, and W. S. U'Ren, secretary, drew a bill for the people to initiate that should enable them to make their own nominations for office and thus knock out the party machines. While this was doing, a railroad planned referendum to delay a state road which the Chamber of Commerce wanted, and the Chamber, in alarm, threatened an initiative for maximum rate bill. That settled the railroad, pleased the business men and showed *them* the use of the new tool. And when, in July, 1903, a circuit court declared the "I. & R." unconstitutional, there was backing for the tool. U'Ren was able to get Senator Mitchell, Brownell, and eight other political and influential corporation attorneys to appear before the Supreme Court, to defend the "I. & R.," which was sweepingly upheld.

The Direct Primary Bill was passed by the people in JUNE, 1904,

56,000 to 16,000. A local option liquor bill was passed by initiative at the same time, and in November several counties and many precincts went "dry." U'Ren had nothing to do with this last, but he did have very much to do with another important enactment—the choice of U. S. Senators by direct vote of the people.

This radical reform was achieved without secrecy, but yet without much public discussion. It was a bomb planted deep in the Direct Primary Bill, and U'Ren planted it—with the help of Mitchell, Brownell, Bourne and two or three editors of newspapers. The idea occurred to U'Ren to write into the Primary bill a clause: that candidates for nomination for the Legislature "*may*" pledge themselves to vote for or against the people's choice for United States Senators, "regardless of personal or party preference." Mitchell helped to draw the clause, now famous as Statement No. 1, which legislators might sign, and he expected to be and, if Heney hadn't caught him grafting, he would have been elected on it without having to bribe legislators. U'Ren would have helped him. As it happened, Mulkey (for a short term of six weeks) and Bourne were the first Senators elected under the amazing law which hardly anybody but U'Ren realized beforehand the full effect of.

That Jonathan Bourne, Jr., should have been the first product of the popular election of Senators has been used to disparage this whole Oregon movement, but Bourne had backed all these reforms with work and money, and U'Ren says he is sincerely for them. But U'Ren tried to get another man to run, and turned to Bourne when he was convinced that, to establish Statement No. 1 as a custom in Oregon, the first candidate must be a man rich enough to fight fire with fire if the legislators should be bribed to go back on their pledges. So, you see, U'Ren was still thinking only of the tool, and he won again. For the knowledge of Bourne's resources and character (and, also, a warning from the back country that the men with guns would come to Salem if their Legislature broke its pledge) did have its effect.

The Legislature confirmed Bourne without bribery and with only four votes against him.

William S. U'Ren
(c. 1909) [104]

The Direct Primary Law settled, a People's Power League was organized (W. S. U'Ren, secretary) to use the people's power, but U'Ren still stuck to tool making. Other reformers used the "I &. R." for particular reforms. The Anti-Saloon League passed a local option bill; the State Grange enacted two franchise tax acts, which the Legislature had failed on; and U'Ren's league put through a constitutional amendment to cut out the state printer's graft. On the other hand, a graft bill to sell the state a toll road, another for woman's suffrage, and a liquor dealers' amendment to the local option bill were all beaten by referendum. But U'Ren and the League worked hardest for and passed, by initiative, bills extending the "I & R." to cities and towns, and giving municipalities complete home rule—more tools. And so—next year, initiative bills were passed to let the people discharge any public officer of the state and choose his successor by a special election (this is the famous "recall"); a corrupt practice act; to make the people's choice of United States Senators mandatory; and, deepest reaching of all, proportional representation. All tools. There were referendum petitions out, also; two against appropriations, one to make passes for public officials compulsory, another to beat a sheriff's graft. But U'Ren was still after the tools.

But will this tool-making never be over? "Yes," said U'Ren; and he added very definitely, "Reform begins in 1910." And one proposition in the list for 1908 showed what we may expect. This was a bill "to exempt from taxation factory buildings and machinery; homes and home improvements, but not the lots nor the farms." Quietly worded though this was, the reform involved is economic, and economic reforms are, as we have seen, what U'Ren is after. And he will get them, he and the people of Oregon. I believe that that state will appear before long as the leader of reform in the United States, and if it is, W. S. U'Ren will rank in history as the law-giver of his day and country.

But what about the man? What about reforms got as he has got his? It must be remembered, before passing judgment, that Oregon was in that stage of corruption where the methods were loose, crude and spontaneous. Perhaps the condition I mean can best be brought home by citing an agreement *written* by Harvey W. Scott, the really great editor of that really great newspaper, *The Oregonian* (and of its afternoon edition, *The Telegram*), one night in 1903. There was a contest on for U. S. Senator. Scott had hopes. Bourne had had them, but he had nothing left but a small minority of legislators. These he owned, however; they had cost him $25,000. Scott wanted Bourne's legislators, so on the last night of the session he wrote the agreement printed below, and Wm. M. Ladd, the leading banker of Portland, *wired* it (hence the verbal errors) to Salem. Here it is:

> "In case I receive Jonathan Bourne, Jr.'s support for United States Senator at the joint session of the Legislature tonight, I hereby agree to use the full power of the Morning Oregonian and the Evening Telegram to defeat John H. Mitchell at the next senatorial election, and to and elect Jonathan Bourne, Jr., in his place.

> "I further agree that if I receive the support of Jonathan Bourne, Jr., for United States Senator in the joint session of the Legislature tonight, that if elected I will turn all the Federal patronage over to Jonathan Bourne, Jr.

"I hereby further agree in lieu [view?] of receiving the support of Jonathan Bourne tonight at the joint session of the legislature, that whether elected or not, I will pay to Jonathan Bourne $25,000 in United States gold coin."

Scott didn't get his senatorship; Brownell threw it to Fulton, but that is neither here nor there. Other contracts like this are in the safe-deposit vaults of Portland, and they illustrate the state of corruption W. S. U'Ren worked his reforms through. And all U'Ren did was to trade, dicker and connive; I've told the worst of it; yes, practically all of it, and it may not be considered as very bad; certainly it never was selfish; but was corruption. So I ask, "Isn't U'Ren only *our* damned rascal?"

U'Ren's house in Oregon City.
(1909) [76]

I put the question to U'Ren himself one day. I was at his home, a small cottage on a point of land that looks up the Willamette River to the famous Falls. It is a very humble home, but spick and span;[15] his wife, a New England woman,[16] sees to that, and she made the rag carpets on the floor, and she makes the warm welcome that is in the air. One afternoon, when the country lawyer was telling me his story, the "wrong as well as the right of it," and we were the midst of one of his deals, his wife looked into the parlour and

[15]U'Ren's three-room house was just north of Abernethy Creek in the Greenpoint addition of Oregon City. It sat on over two acres of land, had 500 feet of Willamette River frontage, and a good view of the falls. U'Ren sold the house and land in 1908—Ed.

[16]Mary Beharrell U'Ren (1868–1949) was born in Indiana, not New England—Ed.

asked him he wouldn't get her some wood. He rose and we went out to the wood-shed; and, as he chopped, I said:

"How well off are you, U'Ren?"

He rested his axe to answer: "I think," he said, "that am one of the richest men Oregon."

"How is that? Have you made money?"

"My earnings average about $1,800 a year. But that isn't I what mean. I haven't any money, but haven't any wants either, not for myself."

"What about your conscience?" I persisted. "What have those compromises with corruption cost you?"

"Nothing," he said. "I never have done a dishonest or a dishonourable thing."

"No, but you have made bargains with the devil to get him to pass your laws. You remember Moses? He also broke the covenants of the Lord, and you know what happened to him. He was taken up where he could see the Land of Promise, but he wasn't allowed to go over into it. Why won't it be so with you? You may have saved the people of Oregon, but haven't you lost your own soul? Won't you go to hell?"

He was looking down while I spoke, and he didn't see that I was speaking half in fun. Evidently he considered the prospect seriously, for after a moment, he looked up steadily at me, and in even tones answered out of his deliberation.

"Well," he said, "I would go to hell for the people of Oregon!"

I believe U'Ren meant that, literally. But is it necessary? Even if it was ever necessary to "do bad things," is it necessary now in Oregon? U'Ren himself thinks not; but the habit of manipulation and compromise is upon him.

Last summer when he appeared at San Francisco to discuss the referendum with Spreckels, Heney and others, U'Ren asked Heney what he thought of backing Fulton for the Senate this year if, by doing so, Fulton could be got to accept Statement No. 1 and thus finally establish the popular choice of U. S. Senators. As U'Ren was giving his shrewd, political reasons for the deal, Heney broke in.

"Ah, quit it," he said. "Fulton's a crook;" and Heney gave facts U'Ren didn't know to prove that the Senator represented "interests, not people," at Washington.

"But it's time you quit your quiet game anyhow," Heney continued. "Go back to Oregon and fight in the open. Tell the people just what you're doing. They'll back you. Give 'em faith; ask 'em to beat that crook, and—run yourself for the Senate. You represent the people up there now. Go on and represent them at Washington in broad daylight."

U'Ren was silent a moment, thoughtful, then he said he felt that his work was at home, teaching the people of Oregon to use the tools they have. And he may be right.

But whether he goes to Washington to make more tools, for the nation, or stays at home to work out his dream of a self-governing people directing their own government in their own common interest, I believe that he should, and that he will take openly the place he has held quietly so long—that of the leader of the people of Oregon. For no matter how his God may judge him, his fellow men will he helped as much by the vision, as by the works, of a spirit as unselfish, steadfast, and serenely pure as William S. U'Ren, the law-giver.

Source: *The American Magazine*—MARCH 1908 [103] and *Upbuilders*—1909 [104]

III

PEOPLE POWER:
1903–1912

5

U'REN TAKES CHARGE

IN THE YEARS FOLLOWING OREGON'S ADOPTION of the Initiative and the Referendum, voters used their new political power to shape a democracy that went beyond what the Swiss had done. Between 1903 and 1912, the citizens of Oregon voted on 108 initiative and referendum measures. They approved 48 of them.

U'Ren and his associates led the way to a new political system that was so unusual that it was referred to as the 'Oregon System' [18].

THE OREGON SYSTEM

Passed by the Legislature

AUSTRALIAN BALLOT LAW (1891)

REGISTRATION LAW (1899)

Approved by the People

THE INITIATIVE AND REFERENDUM (1902)

DIRECT PRIMARY LAW (1904)

HOME RULE LAW (1906)

RECALL OF PUBLIC OFFICIALS LAW (1908)

CORRUPT PRACTICES ACT (1908)

POPULAR ELECTION OF U. S. SENATORS LAW (1908)

PRESIDENTIAL PREFERENCE PRIMARY LAW (1910)

As seen in Part I, the State of Oregon, born 14 FEBRUARY 1859, was by 1880, run by party bosses, by party machines, and by various and numerous grafters. Most people in the state understood this and wanted change.

First, the chaos of the 'voting booth' and the common practice of stealing elections had to be ended. To do this, the AUSTRALIAN BALLOT LAW, was enacted by the Oregon Legislature. Edward W. Bingham, with assistance from W. S. U'Ren and many other right-thinking businessmen, labor leaders, and citizens led the campaign to have it adopted. For more about Bingham and his efforts, see Appendix A.

Bingham also led the campaign to get the Oregon Legislature to enact a REGISTRATION LAW, another important step to ensure fair elections.

Next came the INITIATIVE AND REFERENDUM, the heart of the Oregon System.

On 12 JANUARY 1904, the Direct Primary Nomination League, W. S. U'Ren secretary, was formed at an organizing meeting held in the Chamber of Commerce building in Portland, Oregon.[1] *The Morning Oregonian* reported that the new league would invoke the power of initiative and place before voters a bill, "…which will do away with nominating conventions and make it possible for candidates for office, from United States Senators down to constables, to be nominated directly by the people."

Voters approved the DIRECT PRIMARY LAW in the JUNE general election 56,205 to 16,354—more than 3 to 1 [50].

On 14 DECEMBER 1905, the People's Power League, W. S. U'Ren secretary, was formed:

People's Power League

Organization Is Effected and Officers Are Selected

---

[1] U'Ren's father, W. R. Uren, was a member of the League—Ed.

The People's Power League was formally organized yesterday.... The proposed amendments to the constitution of Oregon were subjected to some discussion, and a set of officers for the first term selected. Ben Selling was made president, George M. Orton vice-president, W. S. U'Ren secretary and B. Lee Paget treasurer. Within the next week or ten days, Secretary U'Ren expects to send throughout the state petitions for signature by voters to aid in securing the desired amendments to the state constitution....

Source: *The Morning Oregonian*-15 DECEMBER 1905 [51]

The People's Power League sponsored five of the eleven measures that were voted on in the 1906 general election. U'Ren explained the outcome of the voting:

> The people approved four amendments to the constitution proposed by initiative petitions; extending the reservation of the initiative and referendum powers to all local, special and municipal legislation; referendum against items, parts and sections of any bill; granting home rule to cities and towns in all their municipal affairs, free from interference by the legislature and limited only by the constitution and criminal laws of the State; allowing one legislature to propose amendments to the constitution (the former provision required the proposal by two consecutive legislatures) and requiring the governor to decide and proclaim whether an amendment is adopted, following the Maine and Maryland constitutions in that respect; granting greater legislative power over the State printing and compensation therefor; enacted two corporation tax laws and an anti-pass law, but the latter was void because the enacting clause was forgotten [115].

U'Ren later explained why regulation of the State Printer was needed:

> ...In the constitution of Oregon we had a provision for a state printer providing that his compensation couldn't be changed during his term of office. That made it necessary to make a law changing it at least four years ahead, and it had not been changed for fifty years....It was the fattest, honest graft in the state of Oregon; $100,000 for a four-year term was a moderate amount for a man to make out of the state printer's business.[2] A good part of it he had to divide up with the boss of his party...[116]

He also explained what went wrong with the anti-pass law to that would have prohibited free or special railroad transportation privileges—which U'Ren himself admitted to accepting in the past:

> ...we took up the anti-pass law and carried it by an overwhelming majority. If failed to operate because—more my fault than anybody else's—in sending the final copy to the printer I forgot the enacting clause. But it had its effect....The next legislature made it and made it so good and strong that nobody rides on a pass there now unless he's a known servant of the railroad [116].

In 1908, the People's Power League proposed four important measures out of the eleven initiatives and eight referendums on the ballot [86].

The RECALL OF PUBLIC OFFICIALS LAW granted voters the power to call for a special election to recall an elected official and elect the official's successor at any time.

[2]$100,000 in 1906 had a relative value of $2,880,000 in 2018—Ed.

The CORRUPT PRACTICES ACT limited campaign contributions, prohibited attempts to persuade voters on election day and when they were at the polling stations, and required the state to bear the cost of providing election information to voters—the start of the *Oregon Voter's Pamphlet*. Appendix C has U'Ren's comments about the Act.

The POPULAR ELECTION OF U. S. SENATORS LAW required state legislators to elect the candidate for the United States Senate who received the most votes in a general election.

The fourth measure was to remove restrictions in the Oregon constitution that prevented a system of first, second, and third choices during elections, also known as proportional representation.

All of the People's Power League's proposals in 1908 were approved by the people.

In 1909 U'Ren took advantage of his political successes and growing reputation and started to work on national issues. He visited Richard S. Childs, founder and executive secretary of the Short Ballot Association in New York. U'Ren told Childs of his enthusiasm for the short ballot principle and the cause of bring efficient government to the people. Woodrow Wilson was the first president of the Short Ballot Association, and U'Ren was elected to be one of its vice-presidents. For more on this topic, see Appendix D.

The general election of 1910 brought to the people thirty-two initiative and referendum measures. When critics complained about the number of measures to be voted on, U'Ren point out that at least half of them were needed because the legislature hadn't given the people what it wanted.

Of the measures brought forth by the People's Power League, a PRESIDENTIAL PREFERENCE PRIMARY LAW passed, but the others, one to create a board of 'people's inspectors' to monitor government operations, one to send a bi-monthly official gazette to all registered voters that would report on state government operations, along with a complicated omnibus bill to enact proportional representation, were all rejected by the people.

In 1912, a flood of 37 measures were on the ballot. One from the People's Power League proposed a constitutional amendment to reorganize state government into a single legislative body to be elected by proportional representation. It was rejected by a large margin.

U'Ren's People's Power League had made so many fundamental changes to Oregon's government in a such a short time that the League, and especially U'Ren, was seen by many, especially his opponents, as a fourth branch of government in the state.

W. S. U'Ren. (c. 1909) [77]

6

U'REN IMPRESSES PRESIDENTS

U'REN'S SUCCESSES IN OREGON made him a national po-
litical figure in touch with important people includ-
ing future president Woodrow Wilson and ex-president
Theodore Roosevelt. U'Ren was on the East Coast in DECEM-
BER 1910. We know this because Burton J. Hendrick wrote about
U'Ren a year later in an article about Woodrow Wilson in *Mc-
Clure's Magazine*.

In a section called 'William S. U'Ren Drops in on Wilson', Hendrick reports that U'Ren had visited Wilson in New Jersey after
Wilson had won election as Governor, but before he was inau-
gurated:

And there were other men from
whom this university president did
not disdain to learn. One day there
dropped into his office a quiet, insinuating citizen from the Pacific Coast.
This was the ex-blacksmith, William
S. U'Ren, the man who is chiefly responsible for the political regeneration of Oregon. U'Ren came to discuss his favorite subject—the initiative and referendum. Governor Wilson had had little faith in this widely
heralded panacea; in his book, "The

Woodrow Wilson.
(C. 1912) [82]

State," he had not approved its workings in Switzerland. He had likewise taught his students, as a matter of theory, that the thing could never work. U'Ren, however, was able to furnish new points of view. Whether or not it could work, whether or not it *had* worked in Switzerland, was not the point; the fact was that it *did* work in Oregon. From numerous other sources Governor Wilson learned much about the practical workings of this expedient. As a result he became persuaded that the initiative and referendum, under particular circumstances, might serve highly useful ends. He does not believe now, any more than when he lectured at Princeton, that it provides a workable system of legislation—that it is a substitute for the representative system. He thinks, however, that it may furnish a tool by which we may get something that we do not possess—a really representative system. He advocates it merely as a temporary agency, a war measure, which, when it has served its purposes, will pass into disuse. He has not yet suggested that New Jersey adopt it in its constitution. Indeed, there seems no reason why he should; for practically everything that Oregon has obtained in ten years by the initiative and referendum Governor Wilson has secured in three months from his own legislature.

Source: McClure's Magazine—NOVEMBER 1911 [36]

U'Ren would meet Theodore Roosevelt when the ex-president traveled to the West Coast by train in the spring of 1911. In anticipation of a stop in Oregon, on 2 FEBRUARY 1911, Senator Jonathan Bourne wrote to Roosevelt's secretary Frank Harper (1882–1971) making arrangements for Governor West, Postmaster Merrick, and the Hon. W. S. U'Ren ("The Colonel has already met Mr. U'Ren and has written to me that he's very favorably impressed with him."), to meet Roosevelt on the train before it reached Portland, Oregon [7].

On 1 MARCH 1911, Harper wrote back to Bourne agreeing to the suggestion that Merrick, West, and U'Ren should board Roosevelt's train at some intermediate point [8].

That same day, Bourne wrote a letter to Roosevelt on the "Oregon-California Train," a letter that must have been delivered to Roosevelt by U'Ren himself [31]:

> I can hardly call this a letter of introduction as you have already met the bearer, my friend, Hon, W. S. U'Ren, and I know you each already have a high regard for the other.
>
> I've written Mr. U'Ren of your Oregon itinerary and suggested that he meet you at Oregon City and accompany you to Portland where I am assured you will receive a very cordial reception.
>
> Regretting that my duties here prevent my being one of the party to receive you…

A letter from Theodore Roosevelt to William Simon U'Ren dated 21 APRIL 1911 indirectly confirms that U'Ren did meet Roosevelt's train and spent time with him. Roosevelt writes that he was happy to hear U'Ren and glad to know that he approved of Roosevelt's speech. He tells U'Ren to see him if he ever visits the East Coast [94].

But there is also direct evidence of their meeting in an editorial Roosevelt later wrote entitled *The People of the Pacific Coast* in SEPTEMBER 1911. Here's an excerpt:

Roosevelt at Eugene, Oregon.
(5 APRIL 1911) [120]

In Oregon I had two small experiences which perhaps will illustrate what I mean when I speak of the development of the cultural life on the Coast, of the development of the kind of citizenship that realizes the need of trying to make life more beautiful and satisfactory for the individual at the same time that we try to make the individual stronger, and to do what we can towards bringing about the reign of righteousness and justice as between individuals.

In Governor West, of Oregon, I found a man more intelligently alive to the beauty of nature and of harmless wild life, more eagerly desirous to avoid the and brutal defacement and destruction of wild nature, and more keenly appreciative of how much this natural beauty should mean to civilized mankind, than almost any other man I have ever met holding high political position....

While riding in the train on the way to Portland, Mr. U'Ren was sitting beside me and answering my questions about the workings of the so-called "direct" governmental system in Oregon. I had been unpleasantly impressed by the preposterous size of the legislative ballot which was voted at the preceding election. Suddenly I heard some bird-song—I think that of the Western meadow-lark—and stopped to listen to it. My companion looked at me for a moment, listened also, and then

Theodore Roosevelt
(c. 1911) [121]

gave the name of the bird. I nodded and remarked that I was really pleased to see that he so evidently cared for and appreciated birds, not only because of the fact itself, but because I hoped that it was a symptom; for I hoped that those who most earnestly led and strove for the success of the radical democratic movement, with which I so heartily sympathized, would never fail to insist on the need of keeping and increasing the power of the individual to get from life that high type of happiness which comes only when neither the ability to achieve material success, nor even the need of doing one's duty, is permitted to atrophy the capacity to derive joy from all that is beautiful, from all that is of interest, in the works of nature and of man. He answered me by expressing his belief that such power of enjoyment and of varied interest would inevitably increase as injustice in our social system was diminished, because the average man would thereby have more time free to devote to the things of the spirit....

Source: *The Outlook*—SEPTEMBER 1911 [95]

Three months later, U'Ren would encounter Woodrow Wilson again. Now governor of New Jersey, Wilson was touring the West Coast as a possible candidate in the Presidential election of 1912. As Wilson was approaching Oregon, *The Morning Oregonian* published this editorial:

The Ideal and the Real

Dr. Woodrow Wilson says he has not discovered anywhere a purpose to supplant representative government with direct legislation. The excellent doctor is therefore heartily and unreservedly for the initiative and referendum, for he thinks that it reinforces, and does not subvert, the constitutional system of our revered forefathers.

If the doctor's thesis is correct, no sincere friend and supporter of representative government—government of, by and for the people—will quarrel with him. But unfortunately it is not correct. When the distinguished traveler reaches Oregon in his swing around the circle he will find here a decided and perhaps a growing sentiment to abolish the Legislature. It has found expression in various ways.

For example, at the session of the State Grange at Corvallis, last week, a resolution proposing substitution of the commission for the legislative form of state government was seriously urged.

During and immediately after every session of the State Legislature we see the radical press violent attacks on that body, with
direct suggestions that it is more than useless; that it betrays
the people; that it is venal, corrupt, indolent, unintelligent and
reactionary; that it legislates too much, with too little benefit;
that it is not responsive to public opinion; that as a system it has
utterly broken down; and that its failures, omissions, evasions
and imperfections can and must all be corrected by the people.
The result is to demoralize the Legislature, and to bring upon
it contempt and opprobrium not altogether deserved.

Dr. Wilson understands and accurately states the true function
of direct legislation: but he has yet to learn how it works in its
free-and-easy form. In Oregon as everyone knows, there are two
Legislatures, one at Salem and one in Oregon City, in U'Ren's
hat. There should be one Legislature and one court of popular
appeal from the Legislature whenever it shall fail in its duty—to
the people themselves. Such a government would be ideal. It is
the kind of government Dr. Wilson and every other good citizen
wants. But who will say that we have it in Oregon?

Source: *The Morning Oregonian*—15 MAY 1911 [57]

U'REN FIRST GAINS GOV. WILSON'S EAR

Oregon City Man Journeys
Over State Line to Out-
wit Democrats.

VISITOR IS IMPRESSED

Prediction Made That Time Will
Come When Nation Will Follow
Oregon's Example—Mind Is
Open on Judiciary Recall.

When Wilson was headed towards
Oregon, the man wearing that hat
took action. The following excerpt is
from the 18 MAY 1911 edition of *The
Morning Oregonian*:

Medford, Or., May 17. (Special)
W. S. U'Ren has stolen a march on the
Democrats of Oregon. Woodrow Wilson, possible presidential candidate
for president next year on the Democratic ticket, has been roped and
tied by the man from Oregon City,
who quietly slipped down over the

California line today and is now personally conducting the visitor into "our midst."

When Governor Wilson's train rolls into the depot at Portland, Mr. U'Ren will not be in evidence. His plan fulfilled, he will quietly drop off the train at Oregon City and have nothing to say for publication. But Governor Wilson will have been informed on the political situation in the state and will know how to greet and what to say to certain of the prominent ones in political circles.

U'Ren Is Much at Home.

Quietly with no word to any of his friends, Mr. U'Ren left Oregon City last night and journeyed south. He traveled to Hornbrook Cal., and there swung aboard Mr. Wilson's train and made himself very much at home in the Governor's drawing-room.

"Just for a friendly chat," explained Mr. U'Ren this afternoon, but those who follow his career are wondering just what he told Governor Wilson and what effect it will have when the Democrats of the state find out about it. The result of his "friendly visit" may be manifest before the Governor leaves the state.

"So this is Oregon," commented Governor Wilson this afternoon as his train rolled over the Oregon line and for the first time he found himself within the boundaries of the state, the laws of which he took occasion to laud in his inaugural address last fall in New Jersey.

New Jersey Follows Example.

"I am very glad to be here, and shall enjoy my stay with you very much indeed. For years I have watched this state and I am very glad that I am to meet your representative men and become acquainted first-hand.

"You may tell the people of Oregon," Mr. Wilson added to the representative of The Oregonian, who met the train at the state line, "that I feel they have done a great deal in developing the movement of popular government throughout the country. The state enjoys an enviable reputation for progressive laws and the politicians the country over have their eyes turned this way. We of New Jersey have adopted many of your laws and hope later to secure the initiative and referendum.

"The laws of recent years adopted in this state seem to me to point the direction which the nation must also take before we have completed our regeneration of a government which has suffered so seriously and so long from private management and selfish organization. Primary laws should be extended to every elective office and to the selection of every committee or official in order that the people may once for all take charge of their own affairs.

Wider Referendum Predicted.

"To nullify bad legislation the referendum must be adopted and is only a question of time until it will be extended to the Nation. The better education of the people, through the various states, of which Oregon was the first, will enable them to pass intelligently upon national measures. In such manner will popular government be lifted from the ranks of theory to actuality and a democracy which represents the will of the people be established."

§ § §

Oregon Law to Be Studied.

"While I am in Oregon," continued Mr. Wilson, "I intend to study at first hand the workings of the initiative and referendum. I believe that this law is really a solution of popular government, as the lawmakers know that the people elect them can at any moment take the lawmaking back into their own hands. Representatives working in the shadow of such law are persuaded to keep in line."

"New Jersey will also hold a primary election in the Spring to express a preference for Presidential candidates and will instruct the state delegation how to vote at the convention. This is one of the provisions of our primary law and I feel that it is good."

"Will you carry your state at this election?" he was asked.

"I would not be at all surprised," he answered.

Governor Wilson while passing through the Rogue River Valley constantly commented upon the beauties of the valley, which at this season of the year is perhaps more beautiful than at any other season. Expressed a great desire to reach Portland and get into immediate touch with conditions in the state.

At Medford Governor Wilson was met by a large number of businessmen who greeted him as "Our next President." The Rogue River University Club had a large delegation to meet him. He was asked to deliver a five-minute address, but asked to be excused as he has a severe cold and his voice is strained from speaking.

Source: *The Morning Oregonian*—18 MAY 1911 [59]

Of keen interest is what Wilson said in his speech to the Portland Commercial Club. This is an excerpt from the book *Woodrow Wilson: His Career, His Statesmanship, and His Public Policies*:

Once when Governor Wilson was accused of exceeding his constitutional rights on account of the pressure which he brought to bear on the Legislature, he simply read to his accuser this section of the New Jersey constitution:

"The Governor shall communicate by message to the Legislature at the opening of each session, and at such other times as he may deem necessary, the condition of the State, and recommend such measures as he may deem expedient."

And then the Governor said: "Inasmuch as it is next to impossible to determine who is running the legislature from the inside, there is an instinctive desire that there should be some force directing and leading it from the outside; some force which shall be obvious and therefore responsible, open to the view of everybody and subject only to the restraints of public opinion. Public opinion must by hook or crook get into the business. If it can not get into it through committee-rooms, it may possibly get into it through executive leadership. If these things don't work the Initiative and Referendum will."

"And that is exactly where some of your friends believe that you are making a mistake in regard to the Initiative and Referendum," I interrupted.

"No one proposes to substitute the Initiative and Referendum for our present methods of legislation, but everybody perceives that as legislation is now managed, public opinion cannot reach it. The Initiative and Referendum is a means of lodging in the people an instrument of control, of which the legislators shall at all times be conscious.

"My visit to Oregon and my observation at first hand of the direct legislation law there has not only convinced me of its success as a practical measure but also forced upon me the conclusion that it is a conservative rather than a radical force. The preparation necessary to the proper operation of the law induces calm reflection."

"Will this not be an efficient means of safeguarding the editing of bills by reducing the number of loop-hole measures, whose authors will fear the use of the Initiative or the outcome of the Referendum?"

"I knew where a great many of the measures of the New Jersey Legislature originated until the last session. They were drawn up in the offices of certain corporation lawyers. That is where they were drawn up, almost invariably, and these gentlemen objected to anybody else drawing them up. They objected to having an ordinary citizen, not connected with a big corporation, assume to suggest a bill.

"Nearly all bills are privately edited. When I was in Portland, *The Oregonian* announced that there were two legislatures in the State: one at Salem, and the other under W. S. U'Ren's hat (the originator of the Oregon system). The implication was that it was most undesirable to have a legislature under Mr. U'ren's hat. After this I remarked in an address before the Portland Commercial Club, that I would prefer legislation drafted under W. S. U'Ren's hat, or under any honest man's or fearless leader's hat, to laws drafted under God knows whose hat."

Source: Woodrow Wilson: His Career,
His Statesmanship, and His Public Policies—1912 [39]

In 1913, Wilson published a collection of excerpts from speeches he had made during his successful 1912 United States presidential election campaign titled *The New Freedom: A Call for the Emancipation of the Generous Energies of a People*. In chapter ten, he explained more about the comments he made in Portland about U'Ren's hat:

When I was in Oregon, not many months ago, I had some very interesting conversations with Mr. U'Ren, who is the father of what is called the Oregon System, a system by which he has put bosses out of business. He is a member of a group of public-spirited men who, whenever they cannot get what they want through the legislature, draw up a bill and submit it to the people, by means of the initiative, and generally get what they want. The day I arrived in Portland, a morning paper happened to say, very ironically, that there were two legislatures in Oregon, one at Salem, the state capital, and the other going around under the hat of Mr. U'Ren. I could not resist the temptation of saying, when I spoke that evening, that, while I was the last man to suggest that power should be concentrated in any single individual or group of individuals, I would, nevertheless, after my experience in New Jersey, rather have a legislature that went around under the hat of somebody in particular whom I knew I could find than a legislature that went around under God knows who's hat; because then you could at least put your finger on your governing force; you would know where to find it [125].

By MAY 1911, Wilson was publicly supporting the initiative, the referendum, and the direct primary.

W. S. U'Ren. (C. 1908) [71]

IV

WILLIAM SIMON U'REN

7

U'REN IN COLORADO

A DEFINITIVE BIOGRAPHY OF William Simon U'Ren hasn't been written yet. It's sorely needed. Your humble editor, besides not being a professional historian, is also not a professional biographer, so the scope of this book is limited.

Many books, websites, academic papers, and dissertations that examine U'Ren recycle incomplete stories and inaccurate facts about his life. This work will use primary sources, now available on the World Wide Web, to share our understanding and interpretations of the events of U'Ren's life, some not well-known, some not previously published.

Starting with his last name. U'Ren spelled his family name three different ways during his lifetime—'Uren', 'Uhren', and 'U'Ren'.

William's father was born in 1834 in Cornwall, England. His family name—Uren—had been spelled that way since the 17TH century.[1] Until U'Ren was 22-years-old, census and newspaper records show that his family name was spelled 'Uren'. Then in 1881, when he moved to Tin Cup, Colorado, he changed the spelling of his name to 'Uhren'.[2] Letters written to him in the Hawaiian Islands in 1888 were sent to 'Wm S Uhren'. After

---

[1] Per the *Dictionary of American Family Names*, the name 'Uren' comes from the Celtic Brythonic languages Welsh, Cornish, and Breton. The personal name *Orbogenos* ('of privileged birth') became, in Old Welsh, *Urbgen* and *Urgen*, then later *Urien*; and, in Old Breton, *Urbien* and *Urien* [30]—Ed.

[2] 'Uhren' can mean 'clocks', 'watches', or 'timepieces' in German—Ed.

that, the spelling of his name as 'Uhren' is found only twice in on-line records—once in 1891 and once in 1910.

The next time U'Ren appears in on-line newspapers is JUNE 1890, in Oregon, on his way to San Fransisco. His family name is given as 'Uren', the same way his family, in Oregon since 1881, were still spelling it.

By 1892, he was spelling his last name 'U'Ren'. An apostrophe used in a name usually means that the word has been contracted, typically to make it sound better (e.g., removing difficult to pronounce consecutive vowels). That's not the case here.

Your humble editor makes the following conjecture. U'Ren's original family name, 'Uren', can sound like the word 'urine' —making it a 'funny name'—and this may have bothered him. In his twenties, he changed its spelling to make it sound Germanic. Later, in Oregon, he added an apostrophe and capitalized the 'r' to create a clear separation of the two syllables of his last name. Then he asked everyone to accent the second syllable when saying his name. He used the spelling 'U'Ren' for the rest of his life.[3]

The Uren family is known to have lived in the state of Wisconsin (1859), in Michigan (1861–1863), in the Territory of Colorado (1866–1867), in the Territory of Wyoming (1868),[4] in Nebraska (1870–1877), again in Colorado (1877–1880), and finally in Oregon by 1881.

During their second time in Colorado, the Uren family lived around Georgetown, Clear Creek County, Colorado, a gold-mining area forty-five miles west of Denver. U'Ren worked as

[3]His father, mother, and two brothers also adopted the spelling 'U'Ren' for their last names—Ed.

[4]Advertisements in the The Cheyenne Leader in JANUARY and FEBRUARY of 1868 show that William R. Uren was running the Lancaster Restaurant and Boarding House in Cheyenne: 'Board and Lodging $13 per week—strictly in advance. The table is supplied with every Luxury of the season. Good Sleeping accommodations. Meals at all hours.' [11]—Ed.

laborer in mines, while his father probably worked, just as he did when he first emigrated from England to Calumet, Michigan in 1851, as a skilled toolmaker at or near mines [43] [83].

It seems W. R. Uren wasn't paid for one job. A legal notice in the 18 MAY 1878 edition of *The Colorado Miner*, published in Georgetown, stated that a William R. Uren was the plaintiff in a lawsuit filed in Clear Creek County District Court against sixteen defendants to enforce a Miner's Lien for $3,409.75 that had been placed 7 JANUARY 1878 on the Zillah Lode, located in the Griffith Mining District. He won the case. A sheriff's sale of the 8,000-foot-long mining claim was scheduled for 21 JUNE 1879 on the front steps of the Georgetown Court House to pay the judgment.

It appears the Urens were also merchants while in Colorado. This item ran in *The Colorado Miner* on 16 NOVEMBER 1878:

> New Business House—Uren & Son have opened a Grocery and Provision Store in Silver Plume and intend to keep a first-class place.[5] The store is next door to the Post office.

U'Ren moved by himself to Denver and became a blacksmith's helper in the railroad yards. He also took evening business classes during the winters of 1878 and 1879 to learn bookkeeping and shorthand [43].

By 1880, he was 21, a law student, and a boarder living at 538-1/2 California St.,. His father, mother, and his four siblings were still living in Georgetown. Both his father and his brother, T. A. Uren, gave their occupation as 'blacksmith' in the U. S. Census taken that year.

The *Corbett & Ballenger's Denver City Directory for 1881* listed

---

[5]The town of Silver Plume was adjacent to Georgetown—Ed.

U'Ren as a student with the law firm of France & Rogers [14].[6]
He was admitted to the Colorado State Bar on 31 JANUARY 1881.[7]

U'Ren then moved to Aspen, Colorado and began advertising
his services as an attorney. The 23 APRIL 1881 edition of *The
Aspen Times* ran this advertisement on page one:[8]

W. S. UREN,

COUNSELOR-AT-LAW,

← *Cooper Avenue, Aspen.*

In JUNE 1881, he was appointed Pitkin County Attorney at a
salary of $75 a month, but continued his private law practice.[9]

Then U'Ren, 22, became associated with a powerful figure in
Colorado politics, John W. Jenkins (1837–1887).

An advertisement on page one of the 30 JULY 1881 edition of
The Aspen Times reads:

JOHN W. JENKINS,   W. S. UREN,
District Attorney.   County Attorney.

JENKINS & UREN,

ASPEN, COLORADO.

John W. Jenkins will appear in all
cases in the District and U. S. Courts.

---

[6]Besides having a notable law career, Lewis B. France (1833–1907) was also
a renowned nature writer known for his works on fly-fishing—Ed.

[7]Bar Admissions, Colorado Supreme Court, ID 461575, Archive Location
41364—Ed.

[8]U'Ren would continue to prominently advertise in newspapers whenever
he was practicing law—Ed.

[9]U'Ren was Pitkin County's first County Attorney, serving from 6 JUNE 1881
to 30 JULY 1881—Ed.

Jenkins, born in Virginia, was active in the Republican Party. He fought with the Union Army during the Civil War, achieving the full rank of Colonel. After the war, he practiced law in Winchester and Richmond, Virginia. He came to the Territory of Colorado (which existed from 1861 to 1876) when he was appointed Territorial Secretary by President Ulysses S. Grant in 1874. He served for one year in that role. In 1876 he was a special assistant United States attorney for the Territory. He went on to be a District Attorney in the new state of Colorado.

In the run-up to the November 1880 general election, Jenkins was assigned by the Republican Party to travel the state and speak about, and promote, the official Republican party ticket, which included James A. Garfield for U.S President and F. W. Pitkin for Governor.

Then, on 30 JULY 1881, U'Ren resigned as Pitkin County's Attorney. Two months, later he was in the mining camp of Tin Cup in Gunnison County, Colorado, at what turned out to be the peak of gold and silver mining in Tin Cup.[10]

Please allow your humble editor to briefly indulge in rank speculation. Was U'Ren a political protégé of Jenkins? Did the Republican party machine send U'Ren to Tin Cup to be an operative there? Is it just a coincidence that U'Ren left Colorado in 1887, the same year that Jenkins died?

Gold had been discovered in the Tin Cup District in 1878. The lure of riches was powerful, and by 1881 Tin Cup and surrounding areas had grown to a population of 4,000. Unfortunately for those digging for a fortune, by 1884 gold and silver production had dropped; by 1886 there were only 400 people left in the mining camp, and with 'The Panic of 1893', most mines closed when the price of silver fell 50 percent [87].

[10]High up in the Colorado Rocky Mountains, at an elevation of 10,157 feet, Tin Cup (or Tincup), originally called Virginia City, was forty-six miles southeast of Aspen and four miles from the summit of the Continental Divide—Ed.

The 1 OCTOBER 1881 edition of *The Garfield Banner* contained this item:[11,12]

> The sign—a real neat one—that is placed on the post-office door, reads, " W. S. Uhren, Attorney at Law," and that gentleman can be found in the BANNER sanctum.

Note that U'Ren was using 'Uhren' for his family name. This spelling is found in all on-line documents covering the rest of his time in Colorado.

An advertisement on page three of the 8 OCTOBER edition of *The Garfield Banner* read:

> **Wm. S. UHREN,**
>
> ATTORNEY AT LAW.
>
> TIN CUP, — — COLORADO.

U'Ren's advertisement moved to the the top of page one in the 12 NOVEMBER edition of *The Garfield Banner*. This move is explained by an item in the 19 NOVEMBER edition of the *Tin Cup Record*. U'Ren was now running the *The Garfield Banner*:

---

[11] *The Garfield Banner*, supported the Republican Party and claimed a circulation of 300 copies—Ed.

[12] "The sign—a real neat one—that is placed on the post-office door, reads, "W. S. Uhren, Attorney at Law," and that gentleman can be found in the *Banner* sanctum."—Ed.

> We understand that the Garfield Banner has changed hands—Messrs. Uhren & Newton will run it hereafter. It will be reduced one-half the former size, with a patent inside printed at St. Louis.

What the *Tin Cup Record* didn't report at the time was that U'Ren and his partner, Ward B. Newton,[13] had leased the paper from Joseph Cotter until 1 MAY 1882.

The masthead of the 19 NOVEMBER 1881 edition of the *The Garfield Banner* included the text, "Uhren & Newton, Publishers," and this announcement:

> Joseph Cotter has severed his connection with the *Banner* until the 1st of May next. Until that time it will be published by Uhren & Newton.
>
> We are tired of politics and propose to take a rest from the subject. Our party has won a substantial victory in every state where an election was held this fall, and we are satisfied. Now we will turn our attention to our principal industry—mining.

U'Ren showed his independence during the duration of his lease by writing editorials against Cotter in the matter of road building projects U'Ren felt were bad for Tin Cup but good for Cotter. Cotter complained to a Denver newspaper that he was being abused and attacked by his own newspaper. U'Ren pointed out that Cotter had given up control of the paper, and besides, he was happy to run anyone's opinion pieces, but not as an editorial [25].

'Uhren & Newton' would publish the paper until the end of their lease. A brief valedictory on the front page of their last edition said:

[13]Newton was described in newspaper items as a young gentleman, well-liked in Tin Cup and surrounding camps, formerly of Des Moines, Iowa—Ed.

To-day we step down and out of the Banner's editorial chair. Our work as an editor is done. Good bye! [26].

Five weeks later, *The Tin Cup Banner* published this humorous dig at U'Ren:

A Fat Legacy.

Dedicated to W. S. U., of Tin Cup.

He was little lawyer man
Who meekly blushed while he began
Her poor dead husband's will to scan.

He smiled, thinking of his fee,
Then said to her so tenderly,
"You have a nice fat leg-acy."

And when he lay in bed next day,
With plasters on his broken head,
He wondered what on earth he said.

The Tin Cup Banner [110]

We learned in Chapter 4 about young William's 'violent but infrequent passions' that his father urged him to control. Two newspaper stories showed that U'Ren was still battling those passions.

The first incident was reported on 22 APRIL 1882:

"THE PEN IS MIGHTIER THAN THE
SWORD,"
———
AND EDITOR UHREN IS ALSO
MIGHTIER, WITH A HORSEWHIP,
THAN JUSTICE OF THE PEACE
NICHOLS, WITH A
PISTOL.

On Wednesday evening Justice Spencer was the center of attraction for spectators. A jury of twelve men, good and true, had swore to dispense equal justice in the matter of Nichols vs. Uhren, and, as the disputants were both well known, an unusual interest became manifest. The large office room of the Miner's Home having been secured for the occasion, and mine host Stevens taxed to the utmost to provide seats for the multitude, many availing themselves of a square foot of floor surface upon which to stand, among which was *The Record* reporter.

The Banner man had the day previous, threatened to entertain "His Honor," with the aid of a mule skinner's "charm" of a whip, to which a demurrer had been entered by the 'Squire, hence the unpleasantness.

The case did not go to the jury for a decision until nearly eleven o'clock Wednesday night. After being out awhile the jury brought in a verdict that Uhren was not guilty, and taxed up the expense of the fun to the account of Justice Nichols [112].

The second incident was reported on 7 OCTOBER that same year:

Col. Violet, editor of the Tin Cup Record, and W. S. Uhren, an attorney of the same camp, had a regular stand-up and knock-down fight on Monday. Uhren attacked Violet in the postoffice with two small bricks of bullion. Violet succeeded in thumping the wiley young attorney, after which Uhren apologized and said to a friend, "I didn't think Violet would fight." Violet then proposed that each take a double barrelled shotgun and perforate each other at twenty paces. Uhren framed a tender objection, and thus the matter rests.—Pitkin Independent [91].

On Tuesday, 7 MARCH 1882, one of the proprietors of Tin Cup's Bullion Exchange Saloon, Charles LaTourette, shot and killed Harry Rivers, the city's Marshal, in front of the saloon. After a coroner's jury was empaneled that day, LaTourette was arrested. The next day, a preliminary trial was held. Seth H. Wood appeared for the defense and W. S. Uhren for the state. After testimony was heard and all the facts elicited, it was determined that LaTourette acted in self-defense. Uhren requested the case be dismissed and the court acquitted and discharged LaTourette. Justice moved fast in Tin Cup and the West in the 1880's [111].

One of U'Ren's cases from DECEMBER 1883—First National Bank v. Devenish—took much longer to resolve, as it was appealed to the Colorado Supreme Court, with a final ruling made in 1890. W. S. Uhren and L. B. France (one of his Denver legal mentors) were attorneys for the appellee. It involved banking law and the risks banks take when they accept and pay checks [6].

It appears that U'Ren got into the mining business in AUGUST 1886. From the *Rocky Mountain Sun* in Aspen:

> Mr Uhrin (sic), who had a law office in Aspen in 1883 (sic), and is well known here, is working a valuable property at Forest Hill near Spring creek, and is putting up a large plant of hoisting machinery [92].

More information on his investment appeared in the *Aspen Daily Times* on 14 OCTOBER 1886, in what looked more like an advertisement than a news report:

> The accompanying...[drawing] is an accurate diagram of the Forest Hills Mining district, which lies southwest of Taylor river, about two miles from Red mountain store, The Forest Hill Mining company is now composed of W. S. Uhren and Mr Woll, of Tin

Cup....In the company property Urhen and Woll each own a sixth...[1].

We don't know the outcome of U'Ren's investment near the Tin Cup mining district, but he must have had capital at risk in the venture.

Eight months later, with the Tin Cup Mining District in terminal decline, the last on-line article your humble editor found about U'Ren in Colorado newspapers appeared on 25 JUNE 1887 in Aspen's *Rocky Mountain Sun*:

> Mr. Uhren of Tin Cup, now in our city, was in the early history of Aspen the attorney for this county. He marvels at the growth attained, and regrets he did not make Aspen his dwelling place [93].

We are told in Chapter 4 by Mr. Steffens that U'Ren 'quit' Colorado due to poor health and moved to Iowa, then back to Colorado, then on to California, then the Hawaiian Islands, and Oregon, and back to Colorado. Your humble editor couldn't find any records on the World Wide Web to document U'Ren's presence in Iowa or Colorado between JULY 1887 and SEPTEMBER 1888.

In 1909, U'Ren mentioned in a speech that he had, "lived...a little while in California." This was probably after he left Colorado and before he went to the Hawaiian Islands [116].

His uncle, Stephen Uren (1837–1931), who had come to California by steamer via 'the isthmus' in 1858, was well-established, and well-respected, as foreman of the Southern Pacific Railroad's blacksmith shop and rolling mills in Sacramento by the 1880's. During William's time in California, Stephen could have easily hosted his nephew at the residence that he built at the corner of 13th and G streets in that city [124].

U'Ren's niece, Mabel Frances Childs Parker (1889–1986), reports in a family history she wrote about her grandfather,

W. R. Uren, that William was in San Jose, California in SEPTEM-
BER 1887. There he wrote to his parents in Prineville, Oregon,
telling them that a 'good doctor' had advised him to live in a
warm, dry climate because of his 'weakened lung condition'.
Parker says that William's father sent him to the Hawaiian Islands where, for a time, he was a manager of a sugar plantation
[83].

A columnist for *The Oregon Daily Journal*, Fred Lockley, who
was in contact with U'Ren in 1922, reported a different story.
U'Ren's health 'broke down' and:

> "The doctors told him that his lungs were seriously
> affected and that he had but a short time to live. He
> went to Honolulu to die, but, running out of money
> while waiting for death, he took a job as foreman
> for a gang of Fuji islanders on a sugar plantation
> and kept so busy he hadn't time to die." [43]

While those are colorful stories, U'Ren gave a straight-forward
account of his health in a letter to friend that was quoted in the
MARCH 1898 edition of *The Direct Legislation Record*:

> "I...was formerly an attorney, but was obliged to
> give it up after six years' practice on account of ill
> health—asthma..." [17]

U'Ren, now 28, would go on to live a long, active, and productive life after leaving Tin Cup—elevation 10,157 feet.

Proof of U'Ren's visit to the Hawaiian Islands can be found on
page four of the 2 OCTOBER 1888 edition of *The Hawaiian Gazette*
[34]. An item titled "List of Letters Remaining in the General
Post Office, Honolulu, Sept. 30, 1888." included this entry:

Uhren, Wm S (2)

U'Ren had been in Hawaii, he informed people that they could write him there, and he left Hawaii sometime before OCTOBER 1888, otherwise there wouldn't have been two letters waiting for him to pick up.

It seems likely that U'Ren left Colorado during the second half of 1887, went to California, then went to the Hawaiian Islands until the end of 1888. He was in Oregon by 1889 [45].

A young W. S. U'Ren. [72]

8

U'REN'S FAMILY IN OREGON

IN 1881, WHEN YOUNG William S. U'Ren was starting his law career, his parents left Colorado and moved to the town of The Dalles—on the Columbia River—in Wasco County, Oregon.

The family, along with Byron F. Childs (1852–1922),[1] first went to visit W. R. Uren's brother Stephen in Sacramento, California. Then W. R. Uren, his son Thomas, and his future son-in-law Byron went north by stage to Portland, Oregon, then east to The Dalles by boat.

Frances Uren, along with her daughters Selena and Frances Mary, and her son Charles, stayed longer in Sacramento before taking a ship up the Pacific Coast, then up the Columbia and Willamette rivers to Portland before completing the journey to their new home in eastern Oregon [83].

At the end of 1881, the Uren's oldest daughter, Selena, married Childs.[2] In the spring of 1882, the couple moved to a farm west of The Dalles near Chenoweth Creek. Their first child, Sheba May, was born there 5 NOVEMBER 1882.

Sometime in 1882 or 1883, the Uren family moved to farmland W. R. Uren bought at the 'The Cove' on the Crooked River. The

---

[1] U'Ren's sister Selena had met Childs in Colorado [83]—Ed.

[2] Selena and Byron were married 17 DECEMBER 1881 by Pastor J. D. Flenner of the Methodist Episcopal Church—Ed.

Cove had fertile land at the bottom of a very steep hillside.[3] The Uren's farmed and raised sheep there.

In JUNE 1884, the Uren and Childs families, except for U'Ren's brother Charles, who took over 'The Cove' property and remained in Wasco County where he became a successful sheep raiser, moved south to Prineville, Crook County, in central Oregon [123].

Postcard shows a view of Prineville, Oregon. (C. 1910) [2]

Childs started B. F. Childs & Co., dealing in General Merchandise, at the southeast corner of Beaver and Third streets in Prineville. His father-in-law, W. R. Uren, soon joined him in the business. By SEPTEMBER 1885, the name of the business had changed to Uren & Childs and they had moved to a new store near the southeast corner of Third and Main streets. Their store later moved into the original 1866 two-story wood Masonic building.

In 1887, Uren & Childs were advertising that they were "The Pioneers Of Low Prices":

[3]In 1964, the Round Butte Dam was built filling the canyons of the Crooked, Deschutes, and Metolius Rivers and forming a reservoir named Lake Billy Chinook, and submerging the area called 'The Cove'. A popular Oregon recreational destination, The Cove Palisades State Park, is situated among the towering cliffs that surround the lake—Ed.

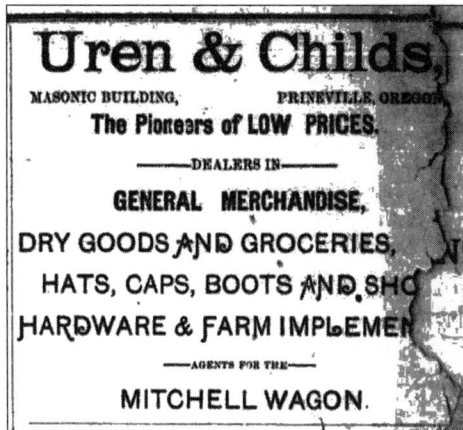

Source: *Ochoco Review*—15 OCTOBER 1887 [67]

In 1889, they moved their business to the 'Brick Store', one of the first brick buildings in Prineville. T. A. Uren was now working in the business [97].[4]

In FEBRUARY 1889, the *Ochoco Review* mentioned W. R. Uren:

> W. R. Uren, formerly of Uren & Childs, spent a portion of the week in town. The old gentleman looks hale and hearty, as if ranch life agreed with him.

In MARCH 1889, the local newspaper reported that T. A. Uren and P. S. Davis left for Portland to buy their spring goods and they went by private conveyance, not the stage.

In JULY 1889, C. P. Uren is mentioned in a local Prineville newspaper. He had recovered from injuries caused by a horse falling on him and that he was passing through Prineville en route to his sheep camps in the Cascades.

In JANUARY 1890, the partnership of Uren & Childs was dissolved. W. R. Uren and T. A. Uren bought out Childs' interest

---

[4]T. A. Uren was also an inventor. On 22 MAY 1894, he was issued U. S. patent NO. 520,096 for a 'Ledger Index' device to aid accountants in finding customers in account books—Ed.

after Childs decided to move his family west to the Willamette Valley. A new partnership was formed: Uren & Son. At some point, two other Prineville men became partners in the business. One was Mark Cary,[5] who had an active role; the other was C. M. Elkins, a prosperous Prineville business man and community leader [68] [107].[6]

In MAY 1890, a local newspaper reported that Uren & Son would be closing and was looking at other investments. Later they advertised their intention to remain in business and, "...try to deserve a part of the public patronage at Uren & Son."

Uren & Son, as a business, appears to have done well financially. An OCTOBER 1890 list of Crook County's top-forty tax payers included Uren & Son. W. R. Uren also had property in Bake Oven, Wasco County, with an assessed value of $6,257.

In JUNE 1894, Uren & Son was again advertising their plans to close their store: "The senior member of the firm wishing to retire from active business...."

The Uren family had prospered in Oregon. It makes sense that after William 'quit' Colorado in 1887, he would eventually join them there.

Fred Lockle, columnist for *The Oregon Daily Journal*, reported that when U'Ren came to Oregon from the Hawaiian Islands, he worked for a time on a ranch near Bake Oven [43]. This must have been the sheep ranch owned by his father and brother Charles.

C. P. Uren, was becoming a prominent sheep raiser with operations in Bake Oven, and then South Junction, Oregon. He married in 1892. By 1894, he had 4,400 sheep in his flocks. By 1900, he had eight ranch hands working for him.

The earliest on-line record your humble editor found of W. S.

---

[5] Also known as Mark E. Carey—Ed.

[6] One of Elkins' businesses was a blacksmith shop across the street from Uren & Son's 'Brick Store'—Ed.

U'Ren in Oregon was in the 6 JUNE 1890 issue of the *The Lebanon Express*. The story was reprinted from the *Ochoco Review* in Prineville:

> For the past two or three months W. S. Uren has been working on a machine intended to be used in shearing sheep, and has at last succeeded in making one that stands the test of practical operation and removes the wool from the sheep as well as an experienced shearer will do by hand. The machine is a simple pair of shears attached to a gearing, the power carried from the driver to the shears through a flexible coil similar to that attached to a dentist's engine. It is claimed that one horse power will drive ten of these machines and that each of the machines operated by one man, will shear 200 sheep in a day.
>
> Mr. Uren left last Monday for San Francisco, where he will have a more perfect machine made and give it a better test. If his machine proves a success he'll associate himself with Uren and Son of this place and establish a factory in San Francisco where they will engage in the manufacture of his invention on a large scale [42].

Another version of the story in *The Dalles Times* added these facts:

> ...Mr. Uren recently had one made in Portland, and last Sunday made a practical test of it which was quite satisfactory. Hand power was applied and the sheep was shorn in 3 minutes quite as well as could have been done by hand....[15]

The need for efficiency the Uren's sheep raising business explains why he was working on a 'sheep-shearing machine'.

No records were found in newspaper or patent records to show that U'Ren's machine ever came to market. About the same time, a man in Australia had patented and marketed the 'Wolseley Sheep-Shearer' which was extensively covered in newspapers. Frederick York Wolseley (1837–1899) made the first commercially successful sheep shearing machinery that revolutionized the wool industry.

While the newspaper stories about U'Ren's machine show that he was spending time in Portland and San Francisco, your humble editor didn't find on-line records documenting his activities in those cities during 1889 or 1890.

There is a record of U'Ren living in Portland in 1891. That year's edition of the *Portland City Directory*, published by R. L. Polk & Co., included this entry:

Uhren Wm S, lab, bds 434 3d.

U'Ren, using the 'Uhren' spelling of his last name, was working as a laborer (lab) and living at a boarding house (bds) at 432 3rd Street (changed in the early 1930's to 1936 SW 3rd Avenue). The building, located in what was then called South Portland, no longer stands; almost every structure in the district was torn down between 1958 and 1962 for an urban renewal project. It stood a few hundred feet southwest of today's Keller Auditorium and Keller Fountain near SW 3rd Avenue and Market Street [89].

The story of U'Ren's next 13 years in Oregon, 1890 to 1902, his meeting E. W. Bingham in Portland and working with the Australian Ballot League, his meeting the Lewellings in Milwaukie, and his campaign to get the initiative and referendum passed in Oregon are covered in Chapters 1, 2, and 4.

In the next chapter, we'll look at events in U'Ren's life after he returned to the practice of law in 1898.

9

U'REN DEALS IN LAW, LOANS, AND POLITICS

WILLIAM S. U'Ren told Lincoln Steffens that he started practicing law again in 1897 as a 'country lawyer'. The *Oregon City Courier Herald's* 1902 'New Year Number', in a story about the town's 'professional men', reported that, "In 1898 Mr. U'Ren resumed the practice of his profession in Oregon City...." Advertisements for his law office began running in Oregon City newspapers in SEPTEMBER 1898.

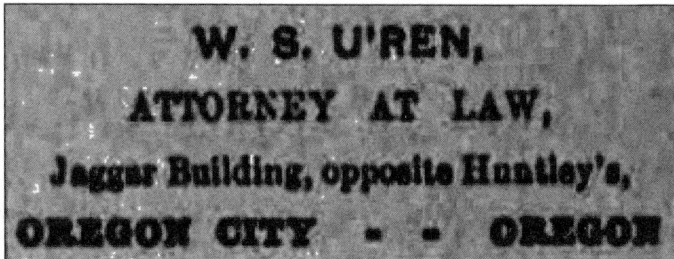

Sometime after 1895, U'Ren's father and mother lived in Monmouth, Oregon, where their youngest daughter Frances Mary attended the state teachers college. Around 1899, they bought a house in Gladstone, Oregon, just north of Oregon City [83]. The 1900 U. S. Census shows that U'Ren lived there with his parents.

In JULY 1900, U'Ren suddenly traveled halfway around the world to war-torn South Africa.

Back in 1895, William's brother Thomas Uren had finally closed Uren & Son in Prineville, Oregon. An article reprinted in the 10 AUGUST edition of *Eugene City Guard* explained T. A. Uren's plans:

> Gone to Africa.—Prineville Review: On Thursday last T A Uren and family, together with his father and mother, left Prineville for Brownsville.[1] After visiting relatives a few days at Brownsville, TA Uren and family will start on their journey of 15,000 miles to Port Elizabeth, South Africa. His father, W.R. Uren, will return to Prineville again this fall to finish adjusting their business affairs here. After that is finished the elder Mr Uren also goes to Africa if he received favorable reports concerning the country from his son.

From *The Eugene City Guard* on 17 AUGUST 1895:

> For South Africa.—Mr TA Uren and family, late of Prineville, who have been visiting his brother-in-law, Mr Slayton, in this city, for a few days, left this morning on their long journey to the South African gold mines. They went to Portland on the local train, from which point they will go to New York by rail, and thence by steamship to their destination.

T. A. Uren and family were in New York on 26 AUGUST. They left there two days later on the steamship 'City of Paris' bound for Port Elizabeth, South Africa, presumably with commercial goods in the cargo hold to start their new business. His father received a letter from Thomas on 9 NOVEMBER reporting that his family was in the Canary Islands and that they were well.

[1] Brownsville is 24-miles north of Eugene at the southern end of the Willamette Valley—Ed.

T. A. Uren, his wife 'Jennie' Uren,[2] and their two children—
they had a third child in 1899—made it to Johannesburg, South
Africa. There T. A. started the mercantile business U'Ren, Cary
& Company and became a leading importer of boots and shoes
in that city.[3] He had three partners in the business: his father,
W. R. Uren, Mark Cary, and C. M. Elkins, his business partners
back in Prineville, Oregon [90] [98] [123].

When the Second Boer War (11 OCTOBER 1899–31 MAY 1902)
started four years later, the T. A. Uren family evacuated to Dur-
ban, Natal. T. A. returned to his business in Johannesburg in
FEBRUARY 1900. He died there from 'quinsy', an abscess of the
throat, on 2 JULY 1900. He was 38-years old [83] [90] [98].

U'Ren's mission was explained in *The Sunday Oregonian* on 22
JULY 1900.

Leaves for Johannesburg
W. S. U'Ren, of Oregon City, Goes to Settle His Brother's Estate

Tomorrow night, W. S. U'Ren, of Oregon City,
will leave Portland for a trip to Johannesburg, South
African Republic. He will go via New York and
Southampton and expects to return in DECEMBER.

Mr. U'Ren goes to Africa to settle the estate of his
brother, T. A. U'Ren, who died there last week. This
brother had been engaged in the mercantile business in Johannesburg for about five years, his associates being his father, W. R. U'Ren, of Gladstone,
near Oregon City; C. M. Elkins, of Prineville, and
Mark E. Carey, formerly of Prineville, but now in
England.[4] All were formerly in business together

[2]Mary Virginia Slayton Uren (1867–1957)—Ed.

[3]T. A. was now spelling his last name 'U'Ren'—Ed.

[4]Mark Cary had gone to South Africa in FEBRUARY of 1894. As of 1910, he
was still in South Africa doing 'big business'—Ed.

in Prineville and concluded to transfer their interests to the Transvaal metropolis, where the establishment thrived. On the breaking out of hostilities last Fall, Mr. U'Ren left Johannesburg, supposing that business would be killed, and that his life would be imperiled by remaining there. He returned in FEBRUARY and was surprised to find that there had been no great interruption to business and that he would have done well to remain [107].

Another report, reprinted a week later in the *The Sunday Oregonian* gave more details about U'Ren's trip:

Going to Settle His Brother's Estate

Spokane Chronicle

W. S. U'Ren, of Oregon City, Or., was at the Grand yesterday morning (25th) for a short time, and then left for Washington, D. C. U'Ren is a prominent politician in Oregon, having figured in the State Legislature. He is now on his way to Johannesburg, and will stop at Washington to get a passport. He expects to sail from New York [108].

A passport was issued to William S. U'Ren on 30 JULY 1900. The application reports that he was 5-feet, 8-inches tall, had brown hair, blue eyes, a light complexion, and a mustache [113].[5]

The next day, U'Ren registered at a New York hotel. He started his ocean voyage soon after that.

The Morning Oregonian reported on 14 OCTOBER 1900 that U'Ren's father and mother had received a letter from him from Cape Town, dated 11 SEPTEMBER, telling them that there was no possibility of getting to Johannesburg [48].

---

[5] At 68-inches tall, U'Ren was average height for his time. The average Civil War soldier in 1864 was 67.7-inches tall. The average U. S. soldier in 1918 was a bit shorter at 67.5-inches tall [32]—Ed.

On 3 JANUARY 1901, *The Morn-ing Oregonian* reported that W. S. U'Ren was back home and passed on his observations about the war. The story says that his trip took him a distance of 30,000 miles [49].

While the article states that, "Mr. U'Ren went to South Africa to settle the estate of his brother...." we don't know what help U'Ren was able to provide his sister-in-law, his nieces, and his nephew. Part of his mission may also have been to look into the status of his father's interests in U'Ren, Cary & Company.

W. S. U'Ren.
(c. 1898) [17]

South Africa probate records show that Jennie and her children remained in South Africa until the estate there was settled in MARCH 1903.[6] She and her children then returned to the United States and settled in Eugene, Oregon [90] [98].

T. A. Uren also left behind assets in Clackamas County, Oregon. On 6 APRIL 1901, his brother William filed a petition with the county probate court asking that Letters of Administration be issued to him to settle T. A.'s estate there for the benefit of the legal heirs, Jennie Uren and her three children [69].[7]

U'Ren, 42, now made two important decisions: first to get married, and second to go into a partnership with another Oregon City attorney:

---

[6]Jennie U'Ren and her children received £2,100 from the estate, worth around $290,000 in 2018 [66]—Ed.

[7]The value of the estate was estimated in the petition to be $3,000, worth around $90,000 in 2018—Ed.

To Marry U'Ren

Mrs. M. E. Moore, for several years a popular teacher in the public schools of Ashland resigned her position last week and left Monday evening for Portland, her home.

It is an open secret among all of the teacher's friends that she is soon to be married to Hon. W. S. U'Ren of Oregon City, well known all over this state as a politician, and who is engaged in law at Oregon City. Mr. U'Ren returned recently from South Africa—Ashland Record.

Source: *The Daily Journal*—16 FEBRUARY 1901 [16]

U'Ren married Mary Beharrell Moore, 33, a widow, in Portland, on 6 MARCH 1901. They would remain married for the next 48 years.

On 11 JANUARY 1901, the *Oregon City Courier-Herald* ran this item:

> "C. Schuebel and W. S. U'Ren, have formed a law co-partnership, and will occupy the office of the former. Mr. U'Ren gives some interesting experiences of his trip to South Africa."

This advertisement for the firm appeared in the 30 AUGUST 1901 edition of the *Oregon City Courier Herald* [73]:[8]

C. SCHUEBEL   W. S. U'REN

UREN & SCHUEBEL

ATTORNEYS AT LAW

Deutscher Advokat

Will practice in all courts, make collections and settlements of estates, furnish abstracts of title, lend you money and lend your money on first mortgage. Office in Enterprise building.

OREGON CITY   OREGON

---

[8] 'Deutscher Advokat' translates to 'German Advocate'—Ed.

Christian Schuebel (1866–1949) was born in Pennsylvania. He came to Oregon in 1878 with his German-born parents. They had a farm near Beaver Creek, nine miles from Oregon City. Schuebel struck out on his own in 1887, working as a lumber jack in the logging camps of Washington, then at Oregon Woolen Mills and Crown-Willamette Pulp & Paper Company in Oregon City. He studied law by correspondence course and at University of Oregon night classes held in Portland. He was admitted to the Oregon bar on 27 JUNE 1897. He was Justice of the Peace for Oregon City in 1896 and 1898. He served four years on the city council of Oregon City, six years as city attorney of Oregon City, and four years as deputy district attorney. Schuebel represented Clackamas County in the Oregon state legislature during the sessions of 1913, 1915, and 1919. Like U'Ren, he was active in reform politics.

U'Ren & Schuebel would last 14 years. From the 1 JANUARY 1914 edition of the *Oregon City Courier*:

LAW FIRM WIDELY KNOWN

U'Ren & Schuebel Among the Leaders at the Bar, as well as in Politics

"What would I say, briefly, was our business? Well, I guess it would be safe to say that we deal in law, loans and politics. And that goes for both Mr. Schuebel and myself."

That is the way Mr. U'Ren, father of the initiative and referendum and usually blamed or honored for the entirety of what is known as "the Oregon system" expressed a summary of activities of himself and his partner, Chris Schuebel, both noted as Oregon City attorneys. As lawyers both men have made reputations that have reached far outside their home state, and both of them have seen service in the state legislature and other political fields. Real estate loans compromise but a department of the firm's business.

Mr. U'Ren, senior member of the firm, is one of those at present seeking the republican nomination for the governorship, and his friends say that they are sure he will obtain the honor. His record as a leader in progressive government has made him already prominent in the state's affairs, and his contributions to the history of past campaigns has shown that he's a power to be reckoned with. Beyond the borders of the state, Mr. U'Ren has been accorded even more honors than at home, and has been eagerly sought as an expert of the initiative and referendum, the recall and other modern policies that are being rapidly adopted in our communities.

As an attorney Mr. U'Ren has shown himself a master of the intricacies of the law, and his quick wit has made him famous in more than many instances. As a public speaker he is also well known, and his forceful yet gently ironical style has made him a prime favorite with his audiences.

U'Ren's peripatetic travels brought out this comment from his law partner:

"…I just celebrated my nineteenth wedding anniversary.…I am planning to go to Los Angeles by automobile this summer. If I succeed in roping U'Ren into staying close to the office for a month, I'll…hie[9] away to…California with Mrs. Schuebel.…"[78]

An advertisement in the *Daily Capital Journal* on 13 JULY 1914, shows that U'Ren & Schuebel had opened an office in Portland

[9]Hie: to go quickly—Ed.

and had added another attorney to the firm, Frank C. Hesse of Oregon City. Hesse was also dealing in politics: a story in *The Morning Oregonian* of 31 OCTOBER 1914 reported that Hesse was talking to leaders of the German-speaking community to get them to support U'Ren in the race for the governorship that year.

The firm U'Ren & Schuebel & Hesse ended at the start of 1915, with Schuebel advertising his solo practice back in Oregon City in the *Oregon City Courier*, while an advertisement in the 4 MARCH 1915 edition of that same paper shows U'Ren & Hesse still with offices in Portland.

In NOVEMBER 1915, U'Ren & Hesse moved their offices to the Oregonian Building, Room 506. On 11 NOVEMBER 1915, the *Oregon City Courier* reported:

U'Ren Changes Office

W. S. U'Ren, formally one of the county seat's leading attorneys, has moved into new offices in Portland, and may now be found by his friends at room 506 Oregonian building. The fact that Mr. U'Ren has moved under the shadow of the "tall tower" need not alarm his political followers....[10]

This humorous note followed in the *The Oregon Daily Journal* of 23 DECEMBER 1915.

W. S. U'Ren, one of Oregon's most well-known attorneys, was in the county seat early in the week. He says that the Oregonian has become accustomed to having him in the same building with it, and that the "tall tower" no longer trembles when he rides up in the elevator.

[10]The Oregonian Building was located in downtown Portland and was headquarters of the *The Oregonian* newspaper from 1892 to 1948. The steel-framed building was the tallest building in Portland until 1911. It was know for its landmark clock tower. It was demolished in 1950—Ed.

In NOVEMBER 1917, U'Ren played along with *The Oregonian* for some local weather humor:

HATLESS U'REN AND PAGET DENY PORTLAND IS RAINY

Usually Bareheaded Pair Don Dome-Protectors for First Time This Season. One Declares Hats Necessary Only Twice a Month in Winter.

It seldom rains in Portland during the Winter months, notwithstanding an impression to the contrary prevailing especially among those living beyond the delightful climactic paradise of Western Oregon.

Mr. B. Lee Paget.

For proof of this statement, there is not only the United States Weather Bureau record which invariably points with more or less dissatisfaction to the usual lack of precipitation, but in addition thereto are the combined declarations of W. S. U'Ren and B. Lee Paget, both of whom follow the practice of going about their business bareheaded.

For instance, it rained last Monday–at intervals, only–and, for the first time this Winter (if such it may be termed) Mr. Padget wore his hat from his residence to his office in a downtown building. That means according to him, that there was a slight dampness in the atmosphere, as it is only upon such occasions that he follows the civilized custom of carrying a hat on his dome.

Mr Padget Carries His.

"I wore a hat downtown Monday for the first time this Winter," said Mr. Paget. "I do not wish it to be understood that I had it on my head all the time, of course: for instance, when I went to luncheon at noon, I did not wear it, neither did I carry an umbrella. I wear a hat only when it rains, which is seldom in Portland and vicinity. I believe I will be hatless on the average during the so-called rainy season about 15 days to one upon which I will wear a hat. It is a great mistake for people to carry the idea about that it rains very much here."

Mr. U'Ren is another eminent authority upon weather. It is his custom to bare his head to the elements, except upon occasions when the sun beats down too hard or when the rain descends too steadily and he forgets his umbrella. That was what happen yesterday, for he was seen about town with a hat on.

Mr. U'Ren Forgets Umbrella.

"I was very reluctant to wear a hat Monday," said Mr. U'Ren when asked whether he had been out in the rain without it. "I forgot my umbrella and, as it did rain a little at times during the day, I put my hat on. Often I carry a hat with me but seldom do I wear it in the customary place. Intense heat or wet weather sometimes suggests greater comfort with than without the hat, hence I at such times wear one.

Mr. W. S. U'Ren.

"There is, however, a very mistaken impression in the minds of some people that Portland and Western Oregon are subject to a rainy season during the Winter; that it rains frequently. I would be false to my city and state were I at this time to remain silent and let that impression prevail. While it is true that we are blessed with fine rains occasionally, which keep our verdure a beautiful green and our atmosphere clarified and fills us with unbounded enthusiasm and energy for our toll, I have proved it to be true that we have many more dry than wet days since I laid aside my hat. We should get over the idea that Western Oregon Winters are dreary and begin to realize that we have an ideal Winter climate here."

Source: *The Sunday Oregonian*—18 NOVEMBER 1917 [106]

It appears that U'Ren's non-hat-wearing choice was the start of a national and world-wide shift in men's fashion. Hat wearing was at its peak from the 1880's until the end of the 1920's. The wide-spread adoption of the personal closed-cabin automobile meant that the formerly functional hat became purely decorative and fell out of favor in a generation or two.

In 1911, President Wilson assumed that U'Ren was a typical hat wearing man. It turns out he didn't wear his famous hat that often.

THE PALATIAL OREGONIAN BUILDING

Not a dark office in the building, absolutely fireproof; electric lights and artesian water; perfect sanitation and thorough ventilation. Elevators run day and night.

Oregonian Building in 1902.

10

U'REN'S OPPONENTS

L IKE MOST SUCCESSFUL PEOPLE IN POLITICS, W. S. U'Ren attracted his share of civil and uncivil opponents, die-hard detractors, and personal enemies. They included close colleagues from his original Milwaukie circle, the editors of important newspapers, such as *The Oregonian*, noted political scientists, and nationally-known critics and commentators.

U'Ren was once provoked to violence by J. D. Stevens, a former colleague turned personal enemy, at a meeting of the Populist Party's state central committee in Portland in JANUARY 1898:

A Lively Meeting

Stevens and U'Ren have a Boxing Match.

The Former Ejected From the Meeting After Drawing First Blood on the Latter.

...The last man in line was J. D. Stevens, of Canby, Clackamas County. As he was about to enter Sergeant-at Arms Fitch asked:

"Who are you?"

Stevens did not have time to explain just who or what he was before U'Ren remarked:

"He is no populist."

"Yes, I am," was the quick retort from Stevens. "Dr. Barton will vouch for me."

"Dr. Barton's word don't go here," said U'Ren.

Stevens glared at his old adversary for a second, then applied to
him an opprobrious epithet. A mix-up followed. U'Ren, stung
by the vile name he had been called, landed his clenched fist in
the face of Stevens, who quickly countered on the right cheek of
U'Ren, drawing blood. Both men clinched and did some little
infighting. Stevens was winding himself up to deliver U'Ren
a solar plexus blow, but Henry Denlinger, of Lincoln County;
L. D. McMahon, of Salem, and Charles Fitch, of Oregon City,
came to the rescue of U'Ren, separated the two men, and the
doughty warrior from Canby was unceremoniously hustled out
of the hall...."

Source: *Oregon City Enterprise*—21 JANUARY 1898 [74]

In 1906, the editors of *The Oregonian* felt U'Ren's ongoing success in passing fundamental political reforms made him so effective—and dangerous—that he had become a powerful fourth
branch of state government:

Now Mr. U'Ren proposes to draft a law regulating the use of
money in political campaigns. Will it be enacted? Of course it
will. In Oregon the state government is divided into four departments—the executive, judicial, legislative and Mr. U'Ren
—and it is still an open question which exerts the most power.
One fact must be considered in making comparisons: That the
Legislature does not dare to repeal the acts of Mr. U'Ren, the
executive has no opportunity to veto them, and thus far the judiciary has upheld all his laws and constitutional amendments.
On the contrary, Mr. U'Ren has boldly clipped the wings of the
executive and legislative departments, and when he gets time
will doubtless put some shackles on the Supreme Court. To
date, the indications are that Mr. U'Ren outweighs any one,
and perhaps all three, of the other departments.

Source: *The Morning Oregonian*—17 JULY 1906 [52]

Seth Lewelling's second wife Sophronia, another U'Ren colleague from Milwaukie and the Initiative and Referendum cam-

paign, leveled sensational charges against U'Ren in a 1908 newspaper story:

U'Ren Posed as Trance Medium

Widow Charges Him With Gross Mismanagement of Big Estate.

Hypnotized Her Husband

Mrs. Seth Lewelling, of Milwaukie, Accuses
Oregon City Statesman of Having Resorted
to Charlatanry to Further His Ends.

By representing that he was controlled by the spirit of their dead son, Mrs. Sophronia V. Lewelling, Milwaukie, declares that W. S. U'Ren, in 1892, exercised a hypnotic influence over herself and husband, the late Seth Lewelling, by which he (U'Ren) succeeded in securing the active management of the Lewelling estate. Mrs. Lewelling admitted at her Milwaukie home yesterday that she did not learn of U'Ren's duplicity until the Summer of 1897, following the death of Mr. Lewelling in the Spring of that year. In the meantime it is charged by the widow that, through gross mismanagement under the stewardship of U'Ren, the estate, consisting of 650 acres of land, was sold by the Sheriff to meet the claims of creditors from whom U'Ren had negotiated loans promiscuously.

In other words, it is asserted by Mrs. Lewelling that between 1892 and 1897, while U'Ren was in charge of the property, an indebtedness of about $28,000 was incurred. This was secured by first and second mortgages on the property, which was still further embarrassed by numerous judgments that were entered by impatient creditors against the estate....

Source: *The Morning Oregonian*—9 MARCH 1908 [54]

The article went on to provide further details about Sophronia Lewelling charges. U'Ren's response was printed the next day. Here are excerpts:

Explains Lewelling Deal

**U'Ren Says He Doesn't Worry
About What Others Say of Him.**

William Simon U'Ren does not appear to be concerned about the published reports relative to his relations with the Lewellings at Milwaukie. When asked for his side of the story, Mr. U'Ren grinned.

"I have never posed as a trance medium in my life," he said. "Such stories are foolish, and all of these things were handed out to me in the campaign of 1898, when I was running against George C. Brownwell for the State Senate.

"I have never bothered other people with my religious beliefs, and I have never been concerned about the religious feelings of others. If I am anything, I am a Spiritualist and I have never tried to conceal it, and I don't suppose the people of Oregon care anything at all about it.

"As for the statement that I used $4000 to promote the initiative and referendum, it is not true. The Lewellings did furnish some money, possibly a few hundred dollars. I attended to their business as if it was my own, and I did it without pay, for I saw that the business could not succeed. The Lewellings had a three-year contract with me, with the option of a three-year renewal, and when the first three years expired, it was they who insisted on renewing the option. No finer men ever lived than Seth Lewelling and Alfred Lewelling (sic).

"In the campaign of 1898, Mrs. Lewelling and J. D. Stevens flooded the county with literature in denunciation of me, and a Portland paper gave me whole pages at a time. But the people of Milwaukie and my neighbors in Oregon City do not believe the infamous reports that have been circulated against me, and I can't help what my enemies believe."

Source: *The Morning Oregonian*—10 MARCH 1908 [55]

Seth Lewelling and his nephew Alfred Luelling—who remained on good terms with U'Ren—were successful business men and community leaders before they met U'Ren. Your humble editor doubts that U'Ren took advantage of them.

By 1909, *The Oregonian* had decided that U'Ren was the leader of a dangerous new political ideology, 'U'Renism':

More U'Renism For Oregon?

As if the things we have in government were not the fruits of long experience and tested fitness, Mr. U'Ren, the Oregon City "lawgiver," is out again with a new batch of innovations and "reforms." These latest changes would supplant in essential principles what is left of the present Oregon Constitution. With little knowledge of the history and processes that produced the old constitution, and with but slight respect for the governmental methods that our ancestors evolved from painful and even bloody striving, Mr. U'Ren now proposes to set them virtually all aside in his plan of "progressive" government. If this be progress then experience is no teacher and history might as well not be written.

The new plan introduces proportional representation—an idealized method of admitting minority factions into legislative affairs and of curtailing or defeating the domination of the majority. It breaks down prized lines separating executive and legislative departments a government by admitting the governor and his cabinet into the legislative assembly and placing that body more or less under his thumb; makes impossible political distinctions and prohibits appointments for party reasons of officers outside the Governor's cabinet; creates offices of three "people's inspectors of government" at a salary of $3000 a year each to conduct a constant inquisition into public and political affairs and publish their opinions at state's expense in the Oregon Official Gazette, of course "without motive or desire for personal or partisan advantage"; creates the office of state business manager, for the ideal purpose of suggesting best methods of state and county administration; gives the Governor appointed of Sheriffs and District Attorneys and power to suspend any local police officer; gives the governor appointment of Attorney-General, Secretary of State, State Treasurer, State Printer, Superintendent of Public Instruction and Secretary of Labor.

Much more innovation is contained in the dispensation from Oregon City, the further details of which will be discussed later as the new plan shall be dissected.

Oregon has suffered enough already without being encrusted further with the U'Ren system. Progress in the state should be in the direction of return to old-tried methods rather than toward new-fangled notions. The world is always abounded with innovators, thinking themselves reformers. But there is very little new or untried in government, and changes should be made slowly, not by wholesale innovations like this now proposed for Oregon. This state has departed already from too many establish landmarks of republican government. The City of Portland, leading the state, has found it necessary to revert to representational political assembly or convention, in order to correct evils of direct primaries; defenders of initiative and referendum, viewing with alarm the dissatisfaction that has resulted from inevitable abuse of those innovations, are calling halt to those who would invoke them and are offering to let the legislature first pass upon initiative measures.

Oregon's old constitution was a nice balance of political and governmental forces. It set up a more satisfactory system of government than Oregon will have again in many a day. Changes have disturbed the balance and now new troubles and new abuses are generated by the new changes. The majority party finds itself unable to express its will and elect holders of the highest offices—those who direct the policies of the state at home and in the Nation. Taxpayers find themselves unable to elect best-fitted men to fill local offices or even to nominate such men. Every minority ism or cranky doctrine can be brought up one election after another, to disturb affairs of government.

The great fault of all U'Renism is that the system panders to minorities at the expense of majority rule. As government, at base and in effect, is majority rule, U'Renism has exerted very disturbing influence. Those who howl loudest for it are minority political elements, whose designs have been advanced by it—Democrats, Socialists, Prohibitionist, certain "reform" factions, disgruntled Republican contingents, and various sets of minority interests whose hope of representation in Legislative Assemblies lies now in proportional representation. All these elements will, of course, support these new dispensations of U'Renism.

Source: *The Morning Oregonian*—16 AUGUST 1909 [56]

The editors of *The Oregonian* warned again about U'Ren's hat in this 1911 editorial:

Leaving It All To U'Ren

The Oregonian will own that it has read Woodrow Wilson's speech at the Commercial Club with a distinct sense of regret and disappointment. The Governor will pardon us, we hope, if we remark that he talked like a college professor, wedded to theories and devoted to abstractions, and not at all like a constructive statesman such as a Governor or possible President should be. It is but little better than pettifogging for the Governor to respond to a bona fide invitation for him to outline his policy, or any policy, or course, or method, by which we may have and keep representative government through the initiative and referendum, with a declaration in effect that as between a legislature at Salem and a legislature in U'Ren's hat, his preference would be for U'Ren's hat. The Oregonian's would not be. Oregon has reached the point where it realizes that it cannot and must not leave it all to U'Ren.

We shall never have restoration of the representative government for which the governor speaks so eloquently by devolving the legislation of a great commonwealth upon one man through the U'Renic method. It is a reversion to the dark ages, when one man was the state, and the people his abject minions. The autocrat then dearly loved his subjects as the demagogue today continually invokes the name of the people. But the people finally got rid of the one and they are beginning to understand and correctly appraise the other.

The people of Oregon have heard over and over of the corruption and wickedness of legislatures under the old method. Many misdemeanors are cited to show that the legislatures were not faithful to the people and that representative government through them was a sorrowful failure. It is not necessary to dispute these extravagant statements of fact or radical deductions of opinions to ask what is to be done now to correct such disgraceful conditions and whether the remedy now being applied is wholly wise or efficacious. The question to be solved now is not the legislative and governmental methods of ten, twenty and fifty years ago; it is the government of today that concerns us and all of us. The initiative and referendum has been here for nearly a decade and is here to stay; representative government is here to stay, we hope. What are we going to do to adjust these two systems and get out of them a workable and satisfactory scheme of government? It is no problem for the doctrinaire or theorist or faddist or stump speaker; but it is a situation that demands gravest and profoundest thought and action of constructive statesmanship.

The people of Oregon are long past the era when they were pleased merely to hear complementarity lectures on the Oregon system; they want to know how to let go of the initiative bear's tail, retaining the desirable features of the initiative and expressing and materializing their will through the representative system.

Dr. Wilson's progress from a vigorous denunciation of venal

and stupid legislatures and an eloquent apostrophe to the Oregon system to his grotesque refuge in U'Ren's hat is not altogether edifying. Will the Democrats of Oregon be quite pleased in 1912 to make the pilgrim's journey to the U'Ren hat-piece in Oregon City in order to dislodge their candidate for President? How does U'Ren's hat suit them for a shrine?

Source: *The Morning Oregonian*—20 MAY 1911 [61]

The editors of *The Oregonian* ridiculed U'Ren in this 1911 item:

Clackamas County scholars are said to be deficient in knowledge of civil government. Clackamas is home of the great apostle of the Oregon plan of government, which is civil and mighty uncivil at times. He might let the radiating rays of his halo illume the minds of his near-constituents.

Source: *The Morning Oregonian*—19 MAY 1911 [60]

The *Mosier Bulletin* took this witty jibe at U'Ren:

A number of Mosierites went to Hood River last Friday evening to hear the Single Tax question debated by Chas. Shields and W. S. Uren. Judging by the applause each of the speakers received, as well as by the weight of argument, Uren converted most of the audience to—Shields' way of thinking.

Source: *Mosier Bulletin*—1 NOVEMBER 1912 [64]

U'Ren support for the single tax was made fun of in this clever poem syndicated in various newspapers in Oregon in 1912:

The New Revalation

U'Ren, the Moses of the modern day,
    Hath lifted to High Fels, his mystic eye,
And heralds forth the latest message gleaned
    From solemn Oregon City's Sinai;
Letting us wandering, baffled tribesmen know
    That which should fill us with sublime elation—
That U'Ren, who hath led us on so long,
    Hath doped us out a new tax revelation.

Far had we wandered, 'neath th' Egyptian code
    Of private ownership of land, which founded
The base of all our state's prosperity
    And led to growth, with certainty surrounded.
Fondly we dreamed of greater, stabler growth;
    But a new vision to the Seer appearing,
Leads him to warn us that the promised land
    Lies farther on, in Single Taxer's clearing.

Neath the old code, by U'Ren supplemented,
    We wandered on, well guided in the light time
By bright cloud castles, and also conducted
    By pillars of hot air within the night time.
Now he would cast those tables down and bust them,
    Whereon is graved our present taxing system,
And carve anew his Fels-inspired commandment—
    The latest revelation of his wisdom.

Oh, "Moses," we have followed you some seasons,
    And were beginning to learn how to take them—
The laws by which you strove to lead from Egypt,
    But now alack you're planning to remake them.
Some of the dope you carried to adoption
    Might, after all, be quite the part of wisdom,
But the thin soup of Single Tax doth drive me
    To hug the fleshpots of our present system.

Dean Collins [12]

Some opponents of 'direct democracy' reforms thought that such measures were not progress, but rather a step backwards in the world's political progress. Charles M. Hollingsworth spelled out his concerns in his 1912 paper "*The So-Called Progressive Movement: Its Real Nature, Causes and Significance*":

...It does not alter this fact to say that the movement is directed against an alleged perversion of the representative system to a class government of the opposite kind, controlled by, and for the benefit of, the large economic interests. Even on that contention, it is only a substitution for one kind of class government of another kind, in some respects less efficient and less stable, and really less democratic. I say less democratic, for, as will presently be shown, it seeks to accomplish its ends, in any state or in the nation, by having the "people" vote plenary, largely arbitrary, powers into the hands of single individuals.

These willing individuals, the real originators and promoters of the movement, take care to declare that they are not bosses or dictators but only leaders of the "people." But that is precisely the literal meaning of the word demagogue, compounded of two Greek words meaning "the common people" and "to lead." And if there is deserved odium attached to this term it is due to the character and conduct of those who have assumed the office....

...Notwithstanding all the claims that are made for the "progressive" reforms in the name and on behalf of the "people," as one which restores them to power, it is in its actual working out really the first step of a revolution to the most narrowly restricted of all forms of government, namely, the arbitrary personal rule of a single individual. On this point decisive evidence may readily be cited from the promoters of the movement themselves.

While Senator Bourne has been almost the sole propagandist in the eastern sections of the country of Oregon's system of "progressive" reforms, it is Mr. W. S. U'Ren, of that state, who is known in that section as the father and chief apostle of the system.

In an interview published in the New York Herald of SEPTEMBER 10, 1911, Mr. U'Ren told how, as the result of a ten-years' campaign of agitation and "educating up to it," "we got the question of amending the constitution to include the initiative and referendum submitted to the people, and the people of Oregon voted for it." And "just as soon as we got the initiative and referendum through we organized the 'People's Power League' to back up measures we wanted the people to vote on."

"Do the people of Oregon always vote the way you want them to?" I asked.

"They always have thus far," replied U'Ren modestly.

"I began to understand, then," says the interviewer, "what the Portland Oregonian meant when it remarked editorially that 'Oregon has two legislatures, one at Salem and one under Mr. U'Ren's hat.' "

Now, this may be in its way government for the "people," as all government is to a certain extent; but it is certainly putting a severe strain on the meaning of terms to call it, pre-eminently, government of the people or by the people, or to apply to it the descriptive phrase, "restoring government to the people." So far as it is put into effect it is personal, one-man government...."

Source: *The Initiative, Referendum and Recall*—1912 [38]

In this editorial, *The Oregonian* continued to be an outspoken voice against U'Ren and what it called his U'Renic ways:

A Voice From the U'Renic Tomb

The Oregonian hears again today from Mr. U'Ren, who abandons the championship of his own failing cause to adopt the old device of abusing the opposition. The illumination of journalistic or personal records is indeed a more or less fruitful pastime. If The Oregonian should choose to retaliate in kind upon Mr.

U'Ren, it might easily offer a sketch of his personal activities since he came to Oregon not agreeable to him; but it will confine itself to U'Ren and the U'Ren measures.

There never was a U'Ren bill that did not contain a joker or trick, or a deliberate attempt to turn favorable public opinion on some important issue into a political asset for U'Ren and his group. It is knavish business; but it is U'Renic. Now the public knows U'Ren, distrusts U'Renism and turns away from him and his system. Well it may. His day is done; he is a mere hireling of a discredited and impossible single-tax extravaganza, and whatever he does or tries to do hereafter will be referred in the public mind to his meal ticket. All the reforms he has proposed through the Oregon system had as their ultimate his present service to Joseph Fels. Thus U'Ren has always smelled his particular from the general weal.

The Oregonian supported the direct primary, and advocated the adoption of the present law; but it complained about Statement One after its purpose had been disclosed, and declared that its results would be to elect Democratic United States Senators. The Oregonian has said, and repeats, that the corrupt practices act is full of absurdities, and we have only to cite the act itself as abundant proof. Here again U'Ren took advantage of a commendable public desire to end the era of corruption in our politics and among the candidates to disfigure the Oregon statute books with the travesty on a correct and practicable statute.

The Oregonian approved, and approves, a Presidential primary law, but it distinctly objected, and yet objects, as the people now undoubtedly object, to the narrow proportional representation scheme—strictly U'Renic in motive and method—that permits the voter to vote for one candidate only and that led directly to the unseemly and unprofitable squabble in a discordant delegation in Chicago last June. It is not true that The Oregonian attacked the three-fourths jury system; it is true that it opposed the extraordinary judicial amendment fathered by

U'Ren in 1910 and fairly bristling with blemishes, uncertainties, twisters and other characteristic U'Renisms. It cannot manifest regret for following the plain path of its duty as it saw its duty then and sees its duty now. There may be profit in hypocritical evasion or easy prostitution of honest opinion and clear conviction; but The Oregonian has never learned the way.

The Oregonian has been the one outspoken voice in Oregon against U'Ren and U'Renism in Oregon. It has seen, as the people now see, that he has sought to capitalize the Oregon system to his own advantage, and that he has gone far beyond the limits of rational and safe form in his recent outgivings. He has descended from his position as a prophet of the people to a mere paid lobbyist for a dangerous and vicious propaganda; and he has confessed that all his life he is aimed at the single-tax and that he procured the initiative and referendum solely with that ultimate objective. If he has given the people more power, others have given them a clear insight into his personal schemings and subtle maneuverings. If he has given us the initiative and referendum, others more wise and less selfishly interested have prevented him from giving Oregon the single tax. If he has given us the direct primary, others have striven against the hostile expression of the inspired clamor, to prevent him from destroying representative government.

If the record of these things done through U'Ren is to be balanced with the record of things attempted by him, but balked by The Oregonian and by the people who have with The Oregonian approved progress with prudence and experimentation with caution, we shall have no reason to be disturbed about the showing.

Source: *The Morning Oregonian*—13 FEBRUARY 1913 [62]

Three years later, the editors of *The Oregonian* acknowledged that U'Ren was a force in the state and couldn't be ignored:

How To Suppress U'Ren

The Oregonian has reason to know that not a few citizens of the state are in complete sympathy with its outspoken correspondent at Enterprise, who would suppress U'Ren and U'Renism and who thinks he ought to be excluded once for all from the columns of The Oregonian.

Mr. U'Ren is a fact and not a theory, nor a phantom, nor a phantasm. Denying his existence may be a pleasing form of self-delusion, but the ultimate results are not at all likely to prove satisfactory. One may shut his eyes, or stuff his ears, or cover up his head, but the everlasting menace of U'Ren is there just the same. It is far better, in the opinion of The Oregonian, that U'Ren should work in the open than in the dark.

Our Enterprise friend is tired of U'Ren. So is The Oregonian. But what is he or The Oregonian going to do about it? The sovereign people have adopted the initiative and referendum, largely upon the suggestion of U'Ren, and there is no way whatever for a disgusted citizen of Enterprise, or anywhere, or for The Oregonian, to prevent him, or anybody, from placing a single-tax measure, or any other measure, or a dozen measures, on the ballot whenever there is an election.

The only way to apprise the people of the nature of a U'Ren bill, or any other bill, is through publicity....

No, the way to extinguish U'Ren is not to ignore him and to say there is no such person, or nuisance, for there is. The only safe course is to meet the U'Ren problem openly and squarely, as often as it is presented, which is too often.

Some day, when the public is more thoroughly aroused to the dangers and follies of U'Renism, and its patience has been tried beyond endurance, there will be an intelligent and successful effort to safeguard the wide-open initiative. That is the only sound and reasonable method to escape from the perennial U'Ren threat and fact.

Source: *The Morning Oregonian*—29 SEPTEMBER 1916 [63]

This excerpt from 'The Foreward-Looker', a chapter in H. L. Mencken's *Prejudices: Third Series*, written in 1922, pokes fun at U'Ren:

...Of all the known orders of men they [forward-lookers] fascinate me the most. I spend whole days reading their pronunciamentos, and am an expert in the ebb and flow of their singularly bizarre ideas. As I have said, I have never encountered one who believed in but one sure cure for all the sorrows of the world, and let it go at that. Nay, even the most timorous of them gives his full faith and credit to at least two. Turn, for example, to the official list of eminent single taxers issued by the Joseph Fels Fund. I defy you to find one solitary man on it who stops with the single tax. There is David Starr Jordan: he is also one of the great whales of pacifism. There is B. O. Flower: he is the emperor of anti-vaccinationists. There is Carrie Chapman Catt: she is hot for every peruna that the suffragettes brew. There is W. S. U'Ren: he is in general practise as a messiah. There is Hamlin Garland: he also chases spooks. There is Jane Addams: vice crusader, pacifist, suffragist, settlement worker. There is Prof. Dr. Scott Nearing: Socialist and martyr. There is Newt Baker: heir of the Wilsonian idealism. There is Gifford Pinchot: conservationist, Prohibitionist, Bull Moose, and professional Good Citizen. There is Judge Ben B. Lindsey: forward-looking's Jack Horner, forever sticking his thumb into new pies. I could run the list to columns, but no need. You know the type as well as I do. Give the forward-looker the direct primary, and he demands the short ballot. Give him the initiative and referendum, and he bawls for the recall of judges. Give him Christian Science, and he proceeds to the swamis and yogis....Give him Prohibition, and he launches a new crusade against cigarettes, coffee, jazz, and custard pies.

Source: *Prejudices: Third Series*—1922 [46]

11

U'REN'S ADVICE TO YOUTH

YOUR HUMBLE EDITOR CONCLUDES THIS WORK with coverage of a speech U'Ren gave to a group of high-school students in 1911. It gives insight into U'Ren as a public speaker and his approach to life:

Self Control Is Subject of Talk

W. S. U'Ren Speaks to Young People at High School Assembly Hour.

Students Hear Inspiring Address

Are Urged to "Rule Own Spirit" Also "Think About Government" — Good Advice Given to Attentive Audience.

W. S. U'Ren, Father of the initiative and referendum in Oregon, talked to the students of the Oregon City high school at the Assembly hour Wednesday morning. Mr. U'Ren never orates, he simply talks along calmly in a conversational tone, and no one tries to get closer to the minds of his audience than he. His subject at the high school may properly be termed "The Ruling of One's Spirit," and he had the closest attention from the boys and girls during his brief address. He said in part:

"The two things that seem to me most worth doing at this time is for each of us to learn to govern himself, and then to serve his country, city, County, State and his nation, and a man's ability to serve his country will be very largely in proportion to his ability to govern himself.

"I read a long time ago the words of the wise man, who said that 'he is who is slow to anger is better than the mighty.' That did not seem unreasonable. Then he went on to say that 'he who ruleth his spirit is better than he who taketh a city,' and that seem to me a very foolish saying. Taking a city looked like a very great thing. Ruling one's own spirit look like a little thing. Anybody could do that. I had never tried very much.

"About two year's after that I did begin to try and have been trying ever since, and now I am willing to admit that the wise man knew what he was talking about.

"I want to urge you to practice this ruling your spirit. It isn't so difficult with your equals, with the boy or the man who is big enough to knock you down after you have said something unpleasant, or your girl friend who can say 'I don't have to associate with a sour face like you,' but with your little brothers and sisters, who can't help themselves, and your father and mother, who must live in the same house with you, and who will overlook many offenses because they think there is some good in you, when you're decently good natured.

"It is with them where the real test comes. Then, as you learn to rule your own spirit, think about ruling the government. You will all have that responsibility in a few years. As we do this wisely, Oregon will be a desirable place to live, and we can, you, and the teachers, and all of us, if we will, we can make Oregon the very best place in the world to live, and we can do that by making the best laws in the world, and obeying the laws better than any other people in the world."

Source: *Morning Enterprise*—4 MAY 1911 [58]

William Simon U'Ren (1859–1949).

V

ADDITIONAL MATERIALS

Appendices

A

U'REN AIDS BINGHAM

THE 'AUSTRALIAN BALLOT' is a specific version of the 'secret ballot'. It was designed by Australian lawyer Henry Samuel Chapman (1803–1881) and enacted in 1856 by the Legislative Council of the newly self-governing Colony of Victoria, recently detached from the founding Colony of New South Wales on the continent of Australia. It was a radical change that transformed elections by making coercion and corruption very difficult [9].

The Australian ballot spread throughout Europe and the United Kingdom, and then on to America. In some places it replaced open voting; in others, it replaced various methods of voting by ballot. It was first used in the United States in 1888 in Louisville, Kentucky. That same year it was enacted in the state of Massachusetts. Most American States had introduced Australian ballot legislation by 1892.

Edward Wingard Bingham led the drive to bring the Australian ballot to Oregon:

The Late E. W. Bingham

Appreciative Sketch of His Life
and Public Service to Oregon

...But his greatest work and the one by which he will always be remembered is that whereby he endeavored to improve the election laws of Oregon, and which are too well known to need any recapitulation here. At the time when he sent out invitations to the electors of Oregon to attend a meeting for the purpose of making reforms in the election laws of the state some of his most intimate friends discouraged him and predicted that the whole scheme would be a failure. But these mournful forebodings were not fulfilled, for the meeting which took place was a very large and enthusiastic one and was attended by some of the most prominent men of the state.[1] The Ballot Reform League was then formed. The ball then set rolling resulted in the enactment of the Australian ballot law, the Lockwood registration law, which Dr. T. L. Elliot, of this city, said "should have been called the Bingham registration law," for it was so largely the work of Mr. Edward W. Bingham, both in its framing and in getting a passed through the Legislature....

Source: *The Sunday Oregonian*—10 JANUARY 1904 [109]

After the successful meeting to form the Ballot Reform League, E. W. Bingham, Secretary, efforts began to educate the voting public about the system. Here's an example:

Ballot Reform Address

Under date of MARCH 21, the following address was issued by the Ballot Reform League to the electors of Oregon—

The perpetuity of our form of government depends upon the purity of our elections. Under the methods tolerated in this state, the elector, in many localities, is practically denied the right of casting his ballot for true representatives of his party or his principles. Nominating conventions rarely represent constituencies. In many instances their sole functions seem to be to publicly announce the results attained by private caucuses of

[1] Although no record was found to show that U'Ren attended this meeting, it very well could have been his introduction to Bingham, a man he came to highly respect. See Chapter 4 for more information on U'Ren's role with the Ballot Reform League—Ed.

political bosses. The same influences manifest themselves on election day in various unpatriotic and indecent ways, and often in total disregard of the rights of the individual voters, who resort to any and every means, legal and illegal, to advance the interests of their employers. Voters are subjected to coercion and undue influences; disorder prevails; repeating is encouraged and bribery is not infrequently resorted to. To assist in correcting these palpable and acknowledged evils and to restore the purity and freedom of the ballot is the earnest desire of all patriotic and intelligent men.

The election—At the polls. (1857) [118]

The adoption of what is generally known as the Australian ballot system will be a long step in the right direction. Its essential features conduce to enlightened and honest political action, and can be adopted by us without trenching in the least upon any provision of our constitution.

The first important feature is: Compulsory secrecy in voting. Nothing can possibly better conduce to prevent coercion and throttle corruption than a secret ballot, cast in the presence of sworn officers only, and in polling places where the voter is absolutely free from observation and beyond the reach of improper influences.

The second important feature is: An exclusively official ballot, containing the names of all candidates for all offices, printed and distributed at public expense. This cuts up by the roots one or the very worst features of our present system—the assessment of candidates for election expenses. There should be no necessary expense attending an election which should not be borne by the public at large. Under the system now prevailing, upon the pretext of collecting money for printing tickets and defraying other apparently lawful expenses, assessments are levied upon candidates, and the funds thus procured are used in any and every way, no matter how illegal, which may seem advantageous to the interests of unscrupulous political managers. Every American citizen who is ambitious to serve his country, and is worthy of the support and confidence of the people, should be by law afforded the opportunity to become a candidate for office without being called upon to make pecuniary contributions for any purpose whatsoever.

The third important feature is that which touches the subject of the filing of certificates of nomination with some designated public officer, whether such nominations are made by conventions representing political parties, or by assemblies, or by a specified number of voters. The provisions presenting these features are calculated to insure good faith and honesty of purpose on the part of nominators and of candidates, and to prevent candidates for public office falling under the control and dictation of secret combinations of political bosses.

The object of this league is to prepare a bill containing these essential features and secure its enactment by the next legislative assembly. This state should of right take her place alongside the other states of the American union which have adopted the reformed system of balloting with marked benefit, and so put a stop to political corruption within her borders. With these essential features of the Australian method engrafted upon our electoral system, the plain and independent citizen will be able to join in nominating candidates to office, and will have an assurance that his vote will not be neutralized by the purchased suffrage of a political hireling.

A strong public sentiment demands this reform. Other reforms are impossible until this one, the greatest and most important of them all, shall have been accomplished. Through it only can untrammeled legal expression be given to popular opinion. To this one measure alone is this league committed, and its existence is determined upon by resolute men until the desired end shall have been attained.

The bill, when drafted, will be submitted for examination and criticism to representative men of all shades of political opinion and of every profession and calling. It is the determination of the league that the bill, when presented to the legislative assembly for enactment, shall represent the mature and disinterested judgment of men whose opinions are entitled to the highest degree of respect.

To all good citizens we send greeting and an invitation to enroll themselves in this league and to co-operate with us. Such information as may be desired will be cheerfully furnished by the secretary, Mr. E. W. Bingham, 74 Morrison street, Portland; and he will also, upon request, forward petitions and enrollment papers to whomsoever may desire them.

E. W. Bingham, Sec.   C. H. Woodward, Ch'n.

Source: *West Shore*—20 MARCH 1890 [5]

The Oregon Republican Party's platform of 16 APRIL 1890 included a plank supporting the adoption of the Australian ballot system:

"...That whereas, the republican party has always contended for a pure electoral system, in pursuance

of this policy, we favor the adoption of the Australian ballot system, and we pledge the republican
party to enact such a law at the next session of the
legislature, substantially upon the lines and of the
character of the act as drafted by the ballot reform
league of Oregon." [23]

On 24 APRIL 1890, the Democrats of the state also gave their
support to the proposed bill in their party platform:

"...We unqualifiedly urge the adoption in this state
of the Australian system of voting, and the passage
by the legislative assembly of the bill drawn by the
Ballot Reform League of Oregon...." [99]

Prospects for passing the bill looked good. But when the Oregon Legislature met in JANUARY 1891, the bill ran into a road-
block. Bingham explained the situation to the public in this
piece.

The Proposed Ballot Law

Salem, JAN. 21—[Editor Oregonian.]—One year ago the Ballot
Reform League of Oregon was organized in Portland, as declared at the time, for the sole purpose of drafting a bill embodying the principles of the Australian ballot system and securing its enactment into a law of this state at this session of
the legislature. On the 20th instant the bill was introduced in
both branches—by Raley (democrat), as senate bill 32 and by
Hall (republican), as house bill 122. They are the same as the
10,000 pamphlet copies of the bill which have been distributed
throughout the state (with some more verbal corrections and
improvements, made by the executive committee of the league.)

The bill is likely to be defeated, and not become a law, for the
following reasons.

Senator Joseph Simon insists upon amending it by tacking on to it some provisions regulating primary elections. He would require the judges and clerks of primary elections to be sworn, keep poll books and tally sheets, and he would also punish bribery and repeating as crimes. He is not willing to introduce these provisions in the form of a bill, but insists upon tacking them on to the league's bill as a rider. In the house a number of influential members, who may be styled the anti-Simon faction, insist that this shall not be done, and reiterate, if it is done, it will kill the bill. Some of them argue that Mr. Simon don't want our Australian bill, and takes this means to kill it. That his real motive is not to wisely or well regulate the primaries, but that it is a covert way to greatly strengthen himself by bringing into service his organized and faithful Portland police. That as long as the primaries are not regulated by law, his police are unable to interfere, except in case of a breach of the peace; where as, if they could make arrests on the pretense of bribery and repeating, they would walk off anti-Simon workers and leave the field clear for their own workers. After the object was accomplished the prosecutions would be dropped. Thus the faction controlling the police force would virtually control the primaries, and thus the conventions and thus the party nominations. The same police force could be employed on occasion to help his-Bellinger-Goldsmith faction at the democratic primaries, and thus control the democratic nominations. Between the two he would be as strong under the Australian system as he is under the present system. They say: "Leave the primaries alone. They are a party affair. It is strange it was never discovered until now they were wrong or needed regulating by law."

Thus, between these factions, our Australian bill is likely to be torn to pieces.

What do the Federated Trades unions in Portland want done, and what have they to say on this subject? Have they no longer any need for a simple, inexpensive way of making nominations and printing and distributing ballots? Have they lost interest in a compulsory secret ballot?

Likewise the granges all over the state? Have they concluded to go out of politics?

Likewise all the business men who enrolled themselves in the Ballot Reform League?

What are you all going to do about it? Do you want your bill passed, or do you wish elections to continue to be conducted as heretofore? If you want the bill drafted by the league enacted without amendment you must attend to the matter now, while it is pending in both branches of the legislature. Mr. Simon had enough republican votes in caucus to make him president, and he certainly has several democratic votes at his command. These will suffice to tack on riders, or amendments, or hang up the bill in committee. Are you all going to stand by and see it done?

Do you think he lacks the courage to do it? Did he lack courage to virtually appoint the two circuit court judges in Multnomah county four years ago, or defeat the nominee of his own party for the supreme court at the same election? Has he never beaten a bill before, or repealed a section of the charter of the city of Portland? As the law stands is he not a police commissioner for life? Need a police commissioner for life have much fear of doing anything?

It simply comes down to this: It is not reasonable to expect professional politicians to want such a bill as ours. It would be as reasonable as to suppose that a cat would want a bell tied around its neck. The professional politicians will kill this bill as effectively as they did the one last session, unless the people who do want it make themselves heard here. If you have changed your minds and don't want the bill enacted, I will go home. If you do want it, I would like you to instruct your representatives and senators here, to please enact the above bills (S. B. 31 and H. B. 122) without amendment.

My address here is care of the state librarian.

Ed. W. Bingham, Secretary of the Late Ballot Reform League of Oregon.

Source: *Evening Capital Journal*—22 JANUARY 1891 [20]

Here's the Federated Trades unions response to Bingham's challenge.

The Voice of Labor

Editor Journal.: Knowing that your paper is read by every member of the legislature, space is asked to say that the Federal Trades Assembly of Portland, representing a membership of 4,780 voters...demands the passage without amendment of the Australian ballot reform bill, as drawn up by the Ballot Reform League and introduced in the Senate and House.

Albert Tozier

Source: *Evening Capital Journal*—24 JANUARY 1891 [22]

In the end, Senator Simon's efforts to kill the bill failed.

A Victory for the People

A good many people imagine that the *Journal* should feel elated over the utter defeat of the Simon amendments, attempted to be fastened upon the Australian ballot law. We do feel elated but not in any personal sense. We feel elated that bossism and failed to engraft its thorns upon a fair tree, which all the people believe will bear good fruit. As the only newspaper at the capital that opposed the amendments, we can rejoice with the people over the results. In many respects it is a result that is surprising. Mr.

Simon's success in controlling legislation in the past has been without a break. He has heretofore controlled both houses and been able to shape affairs for both parties. This session he finds a unanimously hostile house and an uncertain senate.

From a personal standpoint, the *Journal* had no interest in the defeat oh the Simon amendments. From the standpoint that it was the highest duty of the legislature to carry out the unanimously expressed will of the people, it was the duty of every newspaper in the state to demand the enactment of an Australian ballot law, unamended at the dictation of any boss. When any man sought to change that law he was by force of circumstances meant to show his hands and to demonstrate that he was a disinterested friend of clean election methods. That was what Mr. Simon could not do. It was useless for his friends to assert that Mr. Simon was less offensive as a boss than Mr. Lotan. Mr. Lotan was not a party to the contention, as between the people and the proposed amendments. And the result is a victory for Oregon.

Source: *Evening Capital Journal*—9 FEBRUARY 1891 [21]

By 14 FEBRUARY 1891, both houses had passed the bill, and the governor had signed it. The Australian ballot bill, without amendment, became law in Oregon.

In JANUARY 1892, Bingham was helping the Oregon Secretary of State implement the new voting system:

Election Laws and Poll Books

Salem Statesman: The election laws, compiled by the secretary of state, with the assistance of E. W. Bingham, secretary of the Ballot Reform league, have been published and bound and are being prepared for shipment to the county clerks of the several counties, to whom they will be sent as soon as the secretary of state learns the number of election precincts established in each county at the January term of the county courts, as provided in the Australian ballot law. The secretary of state as employed the secretary of the Ballot Reform league, who is understood to be the author of the Australian ballot law, to prepare all the forms of poll books, tally sheets, and other blanks required by said law to be furnished by the secretary of state. These blank forms have been prepared by Mr. Bingham and will soon be printed by the state printer and distributed to the county clerk's of the several counties as required by law.

Source: *The Eugene City Guard*—23 JANUARY 1892 [19]

Bingham also set about educating voters about what they would experience at polls during the first elections under the new system:

The New Ballot Law

At the coming election Oregon will vote under a new plan—the Australian Ballot System—which, by a bill passed at the last session of the legislature became a law in the state. Through the *Evening Telegram* we are able to give to our readers an explanation of the workings of the new system, which comes direct from Mr. E. W. Bingham, who was largely instrumental in framing the new law and one of the most ardent workers to secure its passage. All electors should study carefully the explanation given below:

"The new law will not hinder politicians or party organizations in exercising any of their legitimate political rights, but does take away the monopoly they have had in making the nominations and printing and distributing the ballots, which they abused, and it also requires the voting to be conducted in a room, so that the voters may cast their ballots with secrecy. The old system made it perfectly easy to see the ticket put into the voter's hand go into the box, and thus facilitated bribery and coercion.

Making Nominations.

"Perhaps the principle objects aimed at in the recent law were to place all nominees on a fair and even footing and to compel every elector to vote secretly; therefore the substitution of the official ballot printed and distributed by the County Clerk in each county for the old style or party tickets. In order that a candidate's name shall appear on this official ballot he must be nominated in one of three ways: By some of the party conventions or at a mass meeting composed of not less than 100 electors or by a paper signed by not less than 250 electors, if the nomination is for some office to be voted for throughout the whole state, or for member of congress; but if it is only a county office than fifty electors signing the paper will suffice. In the case of nominations by conventions or mass meetings, the chairman and secretary will certify to the nominations under oath. They must be filed either with the secretary of state or county clerk; but these details it is is hardly worth while capitulating here, as they do not particularly interest the voters.

The Official Ballot.

"The county clerk and each county will print and distribute these official ballots containing the names of all the candidates for each office. They will be printed on two kinds of paper. Those designed to be voted will be printed on a good quality of white paper and will only be obtainable by voters after they have passed within the guard-rail in the polling place on the day of election. The other kind, styled sample ballots, will be printed on colored paper and will be distributed as soon as printed, may be a week before the election, for the information and convenience of voters. They will be duplicate impressions of the white ballot, only differing in the color and quality of paper on which they are printed. The names of the candidates for each office will be arranged alphabetically under the head of each office so as to present to the eye and mind of each voter all the candidates, and he will be compelled, in order to vote, to signify his choice by scratching out the names of the candidates he does not wish to vote for.

Is a Radical Change.

"This is, as you see, a radical change from the old system, and it is hoped it will have the effect of electing candidates upon their merits—their fitness for the office, and with less regard as to how they were nominated. It is thought that fully 90% of the ballots cast in Oregon at the last election were scratched; if so, it indicates that electors were dissatisfied with the nominations made by the regular party conventions. The new form of ballot will be a convenience rather than otherwise to this 90%. The law permits electors to take this official colored ballot into the polling place and booth, and to use it as a guide in scratching the official white ballot, but it requires them to scratch and vote the white ballot with absolute secrecy.

A polling place using the Australian ballot system [85].

What the Voter Must Do.

"On election day, assuming that each voter has already seen one of the colored or sample ballots and has made up his mind how he wants to vote, all he will have to do will be to go to that polling place—that election precinct where he is entitled to vote—and enter the room. It is made unlawful to do any electioneering within fifty feet of any polling place, and he will not be disturbed or insulted as has often been the case in approaching the polls under the old system. He will find in the polling place a guard-rail, and the judges and clerks, and the booths or compartments in which the ballots to be voted must be scratched within the guard-rail, and that only the challengers and a few spectators are present on the outside of the guard-rail.

"He will pass within the guard-rail, and on application to one of the clerks will receive one of the white ballots, the clerk having first taken the precaution to tear off a portion of the stub at the top of the ballot. Without leaving the inclosure the voter will then be obliged

To Scratch Out the Names

Of those candidates on the ballot, for each office, for whom he does not wish to vote, and fold the ballot in such a way that the remaining portion of the stub can be readily detached without anyone seeing how he has scratched the ballot. He will then present his ballot to the chairman of the judges as under the old system and if the judges are satisfied that is the identified ballot which he just before received from the clerk and that he is entitled to vote at that polling place, his ballot will immediately go into the box, the chairman having previously detached the remaining portion of the stub. This stub is simply a margin about two inches wide at the top of the ballot, perforated so as to facilitate its removal and the clerk in issuing the ballot tears off one half of the stub and passes to the chairman and second clerk, who make use of the portion torn off to identify the ballot when it is presented. It is the old principle of indenture applied in elections to make sure that the voter is voting the identical ballot given him and has scratched it secretly.

Can Vote Rapidly.

"As soon as the voter has seen his ballot go into the box he is required to depart. At least ten voters may be engaged in scratching their ballots at the same time, and as fast as they are ready to vote they must present them to the chairman. Thus it is thought voters will not be occupied more than about five minutes in voting. Every candidate on the official ballot has a right to be present personally or by his agent, outside of the guardrail, from the time of the opening of the polls until the count is completed and the returns certified. The new law provides for the appointment of three judges and two clerks for each polling place precisely as the old law directed, and they are to receive the same pay."

Source: *The Oregon Mist*—19 FEBRUARY 1892 [81]

B

U'REN'S NORTH STAR

WILLIAM S. U'REN SPOKE to the NOVEMBER 1910 Single Tax Conference in New York City. The conference was sponsored by The Joseph Fels Fund Commission (1909–1916):

"I read 'Progress and Poverty' in 1882," he said, "and I went just as crazy over the Single Tax idea as any one else ever did. I knew I wanted the Single Tax, and that was about all I did know. I thought I could get it by agitation, and was often disgusted with a world that refused to be agitated for what I wanted. In [1892] I learned what the Initiative and Referendum is and then I saw the way to the Single Tax. So I quit talking Single Tax, not because I was any the less in favor of it but because I saw that the first job was to get the Initiative and Referendum, so that the people, independently of the Legislature, may get what they want rather than take what the Legislature will let them have. We have laid the foundation in Oregon, and our Legislature can not draw a dead line against the people.

"We have cleared the way for a straight Single Tax fight in Oregon. All the work we have done for Direct Legislation has been done with the Single Tax in view, but we have not talked Single Tax because that was not the question before the house. Now that question is before the house in Oregon and we will discuss it. In that State, since we first began our work with the Single Tax as the goal in view, we have confined ourselves to the questions to be voted on at the next election. To do otherwise is to confuse the voters. The Joseph Fels Fund Commission began its work with the definite aim to put the Single Tax into operation somewhere in the United States within five years, and it will succeed in that work." [40]

What Is the Single Tax?

By Daniel Kiefer

Chairman of the Fels Fund Commission

Adam Smith in his "Wealth of Nations" referred to the absence of want in what were then the British Colonies of North America. He also showed the cause of this state of affairs. He said it was due to the easy access the colonists had to the vast natural resources of the country.

These same natural resources exist today and on account of progress in invention, and increase of population, are capable of far greater productivity than in Adam Smith's time. But the workers no longer have the easy access they once had because the land has almost entirely become private property.

The contrast between the distribution of wealth among us today and what it was when the country was still new may be shown by the testimony of many others besides Adam Smith. It all clearly shows land monopoly to be the main cause of poverty and all its resulting evils.

The way to cure an evil is to remove its cause. Poverty can be abolished by destroying its cause—land monopoly—and the Single Tax is the easiest method by which this result can be accomplished. The public appropriation of ground rent will secure the common right of all men to the use of the earth even though existing legal titles be not disturbed. A tax on land values equal to the annual rental value is all that is necessary to make land for all practical purposes common property. At the same time, the abolition of all other forms of taxation would remove another obstruction to industry. The abolition of these taxes, leaving the tax on land values the only one for the raising of all public revenues, is what we mean by the Single Tax.

With the Single Tax in operation the owner of unused or only partially used land would find himself put to heavy expense for the pleasure of claiming title to certain parts of the earth's surface. If he could not or would not make this title a means of giving him enough revenue to pay the tax, he would in all probability drop it and leave the land to some one who both would and could make it sufficiently productive to pay the tax.

Besides making natural opportunities accessible to labor, the Single Tax would be fatal to all the trusts and monopolies that depend either on land monopoly or some form of unjust taxation for support. When it is borne in mind that under it there will be neither protective tariff nor revenue tariff; that there will be no internal revenue duties; no local or State taxes, either direct or indirect on industry or its products, it should be easy to see that the trusts now fostered by one or more of these forms of special privilege will have lost their power to monopolize the industries they now control.

The Single Tax is, in short, the most practical method of social redemption.

Source: *The Single Tax Review*—JANUARY–FEBRUARY 1915 [41]

Single Tax Year Book-Oregon

W. S. U'Ren

In this article I shall deal with the Single Tax movement in Oregon only from the time it was introduced into practical politics, which was in 1908, when H. D. Wagnon, A. D. Cridge and others prepared and proposed a constitutional amendment, exempting from taxes all manufacturing machinery and household furniture, and some other personal property in actual use. Joseph Fels contributed largely to the money expended in this campaign. This measure was advocated and opposed as a step toward the Henry George Single Tax. The vote was about two to one against it after a fairly active campaign in which there was very little bitterness. The total vote on the measure was nearly 90,000.

In 1910 the Single Taxers in and out of organized labor presented, by initiative petition, a "county home rule" constitutional amendment allowing each county to exempt any class or classes of property from taxes, and abolishing the poll and head taxes for the State. It was adopted by about 2,000 majority with a vote of about 90,000. Its success was probably due to the belief of the people generally that it increased their power, and also to the abolition of the odious poll tax. At that time there was no very great or general fear that the Single Tax would follow in counties as the result of the people having the power to vote upon the question.

This campaign was financed wholly by the Joseph Fels Fund Commission. But the Commission did much more than support the County Home Rule Tax Amendment. The campaign was complicated by a bitter attack on the Oregon system of popular government. All the powers that prey were united to destroy the system by indirect attack. Without the literature supplied to every voter in the State, at the expense of the Joseph Fels Fund Commission, there is no doubt the reactionaries and standpatters would have won control of the State government. They would then have placed such restrictions on the use of the initiative and referendum, and so amended the direct primary law, as to have practically restored the old system before the general election of 1912. Instead of that, with the help of the Fels Fund, the progressives not only defeated this attack, but also secured the adoption of the first Presidential Primary Law, which was quickly imitated by so many other States that Wilson's nomination and election over Taft was made possible. No one man contributed more to the success of the 1910 campaign than Dr. W. G. Eggleston. His writings were a very large factor in saving the system of popular government in Oregon.

For the campaign of 1912, the Single Taxers proposed by initiative petition the Graduated Single Tax Constitutional Amendment. The adoption of this measure would have broken up all the great landed estates and exempted all personal property and land improvements from taxes in Oregon. This campaign was one of the most violent and bitter in the history of Oregon politics. No other campaign in Oregon, not excepting the campaigns for Prohibition and Woman Suffrage, has ever aroused so much bitterness, misrepresentation and falsehood. This amendment was lost by a vote of practically 8 to 3 in a total of about 112,000 votes on the question.

At the same election County Single Tax Exemption measures were submitted in the counties of Multnomah, Clackamas and Coos. They were all lost, though in Coos County by a very small majority. In the general stampede against anything that looked like the Single Tax, the County Home Rule Tax Amendment that had been adopted in 1910 was repealed in 1912, though not by a large majority.

In the campaigns of 1910 and 1912, the Fels Fund Commission spent more than $60,000 in Oregon.

In 1914 the Single Taxers proposed the Fifteen Hundred Dollar Homes Tax Exemption Amendment, supported on the ballot by A. D. Cridge, G. M. Orton, Will Daly, H. D. Wagnon and W. S. U'Ren. This measure proposed to exempt for each taxpayer $1500 of the assessed value of his live stock, implements, machinery, merchandise, dwelling house and other buildings, fences, orchards, vines and other land improvements. It was intended especially as an exemption measure for the benefit of the small home owners and the small farmers. This was rejected by a majority of substantially 2 to 1 in a vote of more than 200,000 on the measure. The women voted for the first time at a regular general election. The campaign for this measure was paid for wholly by the Single Taxers of Oregon.

For whatever of blundering there may have been in the campaigns of 1910, 1912 and 1914, the writer accepts full responsibility. He was given practical control of the funds and of the conduct and management of all three campaigns. Joseph Fels, Daniel Kiefer, and Bolton Hall, of the Fels Fund Commission; and C. E. S. Wood and of Oregon, were consistently of the opinion from the beginning and through to the end that the exemption method was a mistake. They held that we should do better and make more rapid progress towards our goal, presenting the full Single Tax philosophy as proposed by Henry George in *Progress and Poverty*, than by any effort for exemptions of any kind, or for the limited Single Tax as proposed by Thomas G. Shearman, no matter in what form the idea might be presented. There were others in Oregon who agreed with them part of the time, and many contributors to the Fels Fund who agreed with them all the time, but the overwhelming majority of the more or less active Single Taxers seemed to believe in and advocated the step by step method.

Apparently the majority in other States still believe in the step by step plan of partial exemption, either for the State at large or for local home rule. But here in Oregon it may be safely said we have learned our lesson. Looking back over the past eight years it seems that many of us have been very stupid and slow to acquire what the Methodists call "a saving conviction" that the Single Tax is essentially and fundamentally a great moral issue. It is not a mere fiscal question of whether taxes shall be paid on one or another kind of property, or whether any class of property owners will pay more or less under one plan than the other.

After our four campaigns here for step by step measures, experience is all we are sure we have. We think we have quite a stock of favorable sentiment accumulated among the voters that will bring them over later with a rush, but the wish may be father to the thought. The young men do not flock to the exemption standard. The hope of saving a few dollars never inspired the search for the Holy Grail. The Sir Galahads do not willingly and knowingly spend their lives saving mere dollars for other men; and the Sir Galahad kind of people are the kind of people who must make the Single Tax a part of the economic system of the world. At no time during our campaign has there been anything like the enthusiasm of the Anti-Poverty Society before the invention of the limited Single Tax.

Judging from the results obtained in British Columbia and other places north of the line, most of us do not believe a mere exemption measure is worth a fight, even if we could be sure of its adoption. The chief result in the British Provinces now seems to have been a boom in land speculation and necessarily higher prices for land. A promise of the same result as to prices was made in the Pueblo campaign, and yet that is not what Single Taxers want or are working for.

We have learned from costly experience in Oregon that Single Taxers must offer a measure which puts our enemies on the defensive. As to mere exemption laws, our foes take the offensive and we are on the defensive. Advocates of a reform worth living for must not occupy the position of explainers and defenders. The explainer and defender in politics is ever a loser. The Single Taxers in and out of organized labor in Oregon are now going after public ownership of all the land rent, both actual or potential. Their measure will break land speculation as soon as it is adopted and will hinder speculation as soon as it receives a fair vote.

We are going out for an economic system in which every man can always make and own his job. With that opportunity ever open, would-be bosses and employers would be ever soliciting the laborer's services, and the laborer himself would pick and choose, instead of being the cheapest of living creatures.

We know from costly experience that the full strength of the moral reason and argument for the Single Tax on land rent cannot be offered for anything less than a demand for its full application. The land rent lords and speculators can present the full strength of their defence, and with all its prejudices, against any mere exemption or site value tax measure for revenue only.

With us, as Single Taxers, revenue is a wholly secondary consideration. Revenue, and more revenue, can be had from a hundred different sources. We want the use of the earth to be free for the sons of men.

We shall never begin to get anything worth while until we tell the people what we want, and all we want, by presenting a full Single Tax measure so far as it is possible to apply the principle under State laws and constitutions. In that day, and in that way, only, we shall prove we have the courage of our convictions.

Source: *Single Tax Year Book (Quinquennial)*—1917 [47]

Joseph Fels, U'Ren's political patron, died 22 FEBRUARY 1914. He was 60-years-old. U'Ren gave this eulogium to *The Oregon Daily Journal* the next day:

W. S. U'Ren Proud of His Association With Joseph Fels

Oregon City: "The world has lost, in the death of Joseph Fels, one of its best men," said W. S. U'Ren of Oregon City this morning. "He was always looking for a square deal for the common man. I know of no other millionaire giving as he did for justice, or primarily to benefit the man working for wages. I don't know anyone else among the class of wealthy men who was spending money so freely to get benefit for the man at the bottom of society. I think the revival of the movement for just taxation, by taking for public purposes the values created by the community, is due more to Joseph Fels and Daniel Kiefer during the past 10 years than any other two men," he continued.

"There is nothing in my life of which I am prouder than my association with Mr. Fels in the Oregon campaigns of 1910 and 1912, not only for single tax but for the people's power in government, and in cleaner politics. By reason of his personal payment of $3000 a year to Mr. Schuebel and myself, I was able to give all my attention to politics and still retain my interest in our law business. I was guilty of an error in judgment in bringing on the single tax campaign in Oregon so soon. I should have waited until the people had established a simple form of government which would be responsive to public opinion and which would be able to spend to good advantage for all the people, the vast public revenues which the single tax will eventually produce. I am sorry Joseph Fells could not live to see the system in full operation somewhere in the United States, but all friends of humanity have reason to rejoice that he lived so long.

"His home life was as simple and plain as that of an Oregon farmer. I think it would not be possible for a man to be more devoted to an ideal for humanity than Joseph Fels."

Source: *The Oregon Daily Journal*—23 FEBRUARY 1914 [80]

C

U'REN FIGHTS CORRUPTION

How Oregon Secured Pure Elections

Corrupt Practices Law Prevents Excessive Use of Money in Political Campaigns.

It Makes Possible Quiet Elections

By W. S. U'Ren

O NE OF THE DIFFICULT PROBLEMS of the people's government is to bring the cost of aspiring to public office within the reach of poor men. In a constituency of 5,000 voters, the politicians say the legitimate cost to an individual candidate will seldom go much below $500, and may even reach $1,000. As the number of voters increases, the cost of the campaign rises until it is soon beyond the reach of any man who expects to make a living, pay his campaign expenses, and save a little from his salary as a public officer.

Yet, for the good of the state it is necessary that no one of its citizens who is otherwise qualified for its public service, should be barred because he dare not risk or cannot spend the amount of the necessary and legitimate campaign expenses. The Direct Primary system brought home to all the people of Oregon the evils of costly campaigns. It was easy to see that a very large part of the expense was productive of evil only, and more of it was unnecessary. But if one candidate or party was allowed to spend freely for hired workers and paid advertising, others would feel obliged to do the same.

Because of the many evils of unlimited campaign expenses, the people in Oregon in 1908 enacted a Corrupt Practices law, proposed by initiative petition. Its basic thought is the reduction of the actual necessary cost of nominating and election campaigns to a minimum, both for candidates and for the state, and then the material increase of the share of that expense to be paid directly from the public treasury. At the same time it is intended to give every aspirant for nomination, and all his enemies, as well as the candidates and principles of every political party, an equal and fair chance to get the voters' attention.

Its first test was in the presidential election last November. Oregon had about 130,000 registered voters at that time. The verified statements of expenses show that the Republican party spent $5,610, the Democratic party, $2,521.81, the Socialists nothing, the Prohibitionists, $453.15; the Hearst party $359, and the candidates individually enough more to make the total amount spent in the presidential campaign $9,367.91. It was altogether the quietest and best ordered election Oregon ever saw.

Law Is Effective

The operation of the Corrupt Practices law was universally commended by the press. Portland is a city of 225,000 inhabitants, but there was not a single arrest for disorderly conduct at the polls, which was said to be without a precedent. At many former elections the jails were not large enough to hold the victims. Before the election there was some criticism, especially by the *Daily Oregonian*, of the provisions against wearing badges, banners, etc., at the polls. But after the election there was no word of unfavorable comment. The news columns of the *Oregonian*, the leading Republican paper, reported "Absolutely new and extremely novel conditions in regard to political workings throughout the state made the day as quiet and devoid of incident as a June Sunday in the country. It was Portland's first

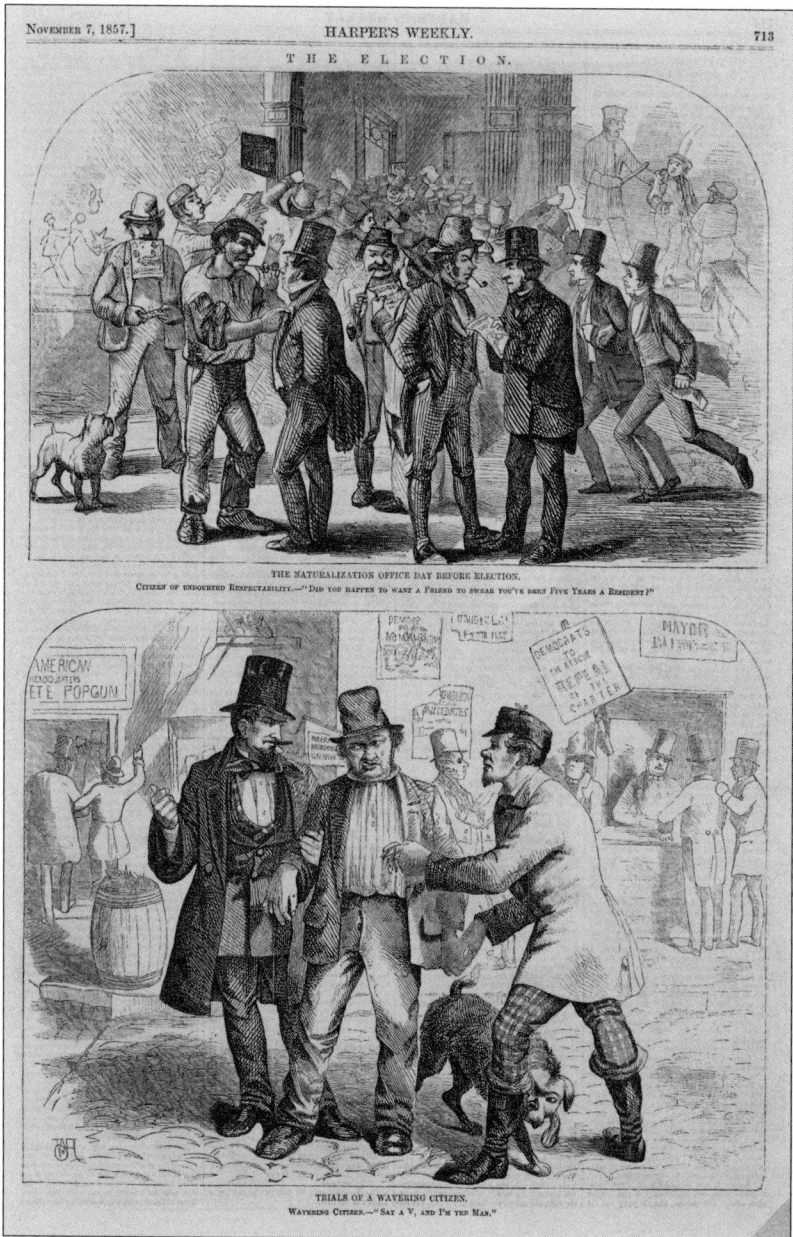

Elections before laws limiting corrupt practices [117].

election under the operation of the Huntley Corrupt Practices law, a conspicuous result of which was the absence of distressed-looking individuals who have been accustomed for years in this city to distribute cards and arguments in the vicinity of the voting place. Another feature was the absence of carriages with flaming banners, lithographs, cards and dodgers."

"Scenes attending the balloting' throughout the state were devoid of great interest. The provisions of the Corrupt Practices act were generally regarded and the usual buttonholing of electors at the voting places was not observed anywhere. Voters very generally discarded campaign buttons and other outward evidence of their party choice before going to the booths, which were deserted except for the members of the election board, the citizens casting their ballots, and an occasional policeman, who was in attendance in case his services were required."

The *Daily Evening Telegram* of Portland said editorially after the election concerning this law, "Not the least gratifying of its features are those which regulate the conduct of political managers, of election officers and of the electors on election day and at the polls. The inhibitions of the act in this regard are based upon the assumption that in the weeks preceding election there has been sufficient time for discussion and determination as to the merits of the candidates and issues. It assumes that election day is the time for untrammeled action, except as the elector shall be governed by the arguments that have been made and the thought that has been devoted to the measures at issue during the campaign. It is the conclusion that with the preliminaries disposed of there is nothing left but to vote, and that this duty should be performed without the annoyance of card peddlers and election-day button-holders.

"Moreover the Corrupt Practices act tends to make the exercise of the franchise a matter of self-reliance; and, incidentally, it puts the crowd of political strikers out of commission. It saves the expenditure of money originally devoted to no good purpose so far as the purity of elections was concerned. We may say with pride, that Oregon has taken high ground in the enact-ment and enforcement of this law."

"Universally Satisfactory"

I could give columns of similar editorials and news statements but it seems to me these are sufficient. The law was patterned very closely after the British acts governing the election of mem-bers of Parliament, except as to the provision for the circulation of some campaign literature principally at the expense of the state. I believe Governor Hughes was the first to suggest that this should be done, and so far as we were able to learn in Ore-gon this law is the first attempt to apply this principle. The operation of the law was universally satisfactory.

Source: *La Follette's Weekly Magazine*—3 APRIL 1909 [114]

D

U'REN WANTS EFFICIENT GOVERNMENT

L INCOLN STEFFENS POINTED OUT in his famous work, *"The Shame of Cities"*, that if ballots were shorter, voters would exercise better judgment when presented with fewer choices. People were regularly being confused by long lines of unrecognizable names controlled by political bosses. The Short Ballot Association was organized in 1909 by Richard S. Childs to agitate for it nationally. U'Ren was one of its vice-presidents:

The Short Ballot Principle
As Officially Defined by The National Short Ballot Organization

The dangerously great power of politicians in our country is not due to any peculiar civic indifference of the people, but rests on the fact that we are living under a form of democracy that is so unworkable as to constitute in practice a pseudo-democracy. It is unworkable because—

First—It submits to popular election offices which are too unimportant to attract (or deserve) public attention, and,

Second—It submits to popular election so many offices at one time that many of them are inevitably crowded out from proper

public attention, and,

Third—It submits to popular election so many offices at one time as to make the business of ticket-making too intricate for popular participation, whereupon some sort of private political machine becomes an indispensable instrument in electoral action.

Many officials, therefore, are elected without adequate public scrutiny, and owe their selection not to the people, but to the makers of the party ticket, who thus acquire an influence that is capable of great abuse.

No. 1. The Glasgow (Scotland) voter has only one name—his ward councilman—to vote for, and he has the best city government in the world.

No. 2. The Des Moines (Iowa) voter has only five men on his ticket, and has the best city government in the United States.

No. 3. The Portland, Oregon, voter has in this year of our Lord 1912, about 100 candidates for office on his ticket; and 39 long initiative and referendum proposed state laws, and 22 proposed city laws—and altogether proposing an indebtedness on the taxpayers of forty to fifty millions of dollars. It is safe to say that all this proposed law making will not even be read by one-fourth of the voters—and no man can know what his rights or obligations may be under these circumstances.

The ballot in Portland was longer, not shorter, in 1912 [27].

The "SHORT BALLOT" principle is— First—That only those offices should be elective which are important enough to attract (and deserve) public examination.

Second—That very few offices should be filled by election at one time, so as to permit adequate and unconfused public examination of the candidates, and so as to facilitate the free and intelligent making of original tickets by any voter for himself unaided by political specialists.

Obedience to this fundamental principle explains the comparative success of democratic government in the cities of Great Britain and other foreign democracies, as well as in Galveston, Des Moines and other American cities that are governed by "Commissions."

The application of this principle should be extended to all cities, counties and states.

Source: *The Short Ballot: A movement to Simplify Politics*—1915 [65]

By 1914, the Short Ballot Association was also agitating for the adoption of "The City Manager Plan of Municipal Government".

The plan was to have the people elect, on a non-partisan ballot, a council of popular representatives, who hire and control with the right to remove, a city manager, a well-paid, full-time, non-political central executive, who appoints, supervises, and removes the heads of all departments, who in turn control the rank-and-file of the administration.

Today, a majority of U. S. cities with a population over 2,500 use the plan, a system its original supporters thought was the most democratic form of municipal government.

E

U'REN'S AMENDMENT

OREGON'S FIRST CONSTITUTIONAL AMENDMENT, adopted in 1902, gave the power of the Initiative and the Referendum to the people of Oregon. Here's the text of the amendment:

Section 1, Article IV of the Constitution of Oregon

The legislative authority of the state shall be vested in a legislative assembly, consisting of a senate and house of representatives, but the people reserve to themselves power to propose laws and amendments to the constitution, and to enact or reject the same at the polls, independent of the legislative assembly, and also reserve power at their own option to approve or reject at the polls any act of the legislative assembly. The first power reserved by the people is the initiative, and not more than eight per cent of the legal voters shall be required to propose any measure by such petition, and every such petition shall include the full text of the measure so proposed. Initiative petitions shall be filed with the secretary of state not less than four months before the election at which they are to be voted upon. The second power is the referendum, and it may be ordered (except as to laws necessary for the immediate preservation of the public peace, health or safety) either by petition, signed by five per cent. of the legal voters, or by the legislative assembly, as other bills are enacted. Referendum petitions shall be filed with the secretary of state not more than ninety days after the final adjournment of the session of the legislative assembly which passed the bill on which the referendum is demanded. The veto power of the governor shall not extend to measures referred to the people. All elections on measures referred to the people of the state shall be had at the biennial regular general elections, except when the legislative assembly shall order a special election. Any measure referred to the people shall take effect and become the law when it is approved by a majority of the votes cast thereon, and not otherwise. The style of all bills shall be: "Be it enacted by the people of the state of Oregon." This section shall not be construed to deprive any member of the legislative assembly of the right to introduce any measure. The whole number of votes cast for justice of the supreme court at the regular election last preceding the filing of any petition for the initiative or for the referendum shall be the basis on which the number of legal voters necessary to sign such petition shall be counted. Petitions and orders for the initiative and for the referendum shall be filed with the secretary of state, and in submitting the same to the people he and all other officers shall be guided by the general laws and the act submitting this amendment until legislation shall be especially provided therefor.

It has since been amended three times:

- H. J. R. 16 (1967), adopted by the people 28 MAY 1968

- S. J. R. 27 (1985), adopted by the people 20 MAY 1986

- S. J. R. 3 (1999), adopted by the people 16 MAY 2000

BIBLIOGRAPHY

[1] *Aspen Daily Times.* *"Taylor Park."* (14 OCTOBER 1886): 3.

[2] Bakowski, B. B.,. *Prineville, Oregon c. 1910.* Photograph. loc.gov/item/2013646990/

[3] Bain News Service. *"Lincoln Steffens."* Photograph. loc.gov/item/2014685703/

[4] Bain News Service. *"Linc. Steffens, 1914."* Photograph. loc.gov/item/2014695906/

[5] Bingham, Edward W.,. *"Ballot Reform Address."* *West Shore* (20 MARCH 1890): 390.

[6] Beck, William E.,. *Reports of Cases Determined in the Supreme Court of the State of Colorado,* VOL. 15. Chicago: Callaghan & Company, Publishers, 1891.

[7] Letter from Jonathan Bourne to Frank Harper, Theodore Roosevelt Papers, Library of Congress Manuscript Division. www.theodorerooseveltcenter.org, ID=o65245, Theodore Roosevelt Digital Library, Dickinson State University.

[8] Letter from Jonathan Bourne to Theodore Roosevelt, Theodore Roosevelt Papers, Library of Congress Manuscript Division. www.theodorerooseveltcenter.org, ID=o216454, Theodore Roosevelt Digital Library, Dickinson State University.

[9] Brent, Peter. *"The Australian Ballot: Not the Secret Ballot."* *Australian Journal of Political Science,* VOL. 41, NO. 1 (MARCH 2006): 39-50. http://dx.doi.org/10.1080/10361140500507278

[10] Chapman Publishing Company. *Portrait and Biographical Record of Portland and Vicinity Oregon.* Chicago (1903).

[11] *The Cheyenne Leader.* "Advertisement for the Lancaster Restaurant." VOL. I, NO. 107 (24 JANUARY 1868): I.

[12] Collins, Dean. *"The New Revalation." The Monmouth Herald* (20 SEPTEMBER 1912).

[13] Department of Commerce, Bureau of the Census. *Thirteenth Census of the United States Taken in the Year* 1910, VOLUME III, *Population.* Washington: Government Printing Office, 1913.

[14] Corbett & Ballenger. *Corbett & Ballenger's Denver City Directory for* 1881. Denver (1881): 507.

[15] *The Dalles Times Mountaineer.* "Items In..." (7 JUNE 1890): 2.

[16] *The Daily Journal.* "To Marry U'Ren." (16 FEBRUARY 1901)

[17] *The Direct Legislation Record.* "Thum-nail Sketches. W. S. U'Ren."* Newark, New Jersey: (MARCH 1898): 19–20.

[18] Eaton, Allen H.,. *The Oregon System: The Story of Direct Legislation in Oregon.* Chicago: A. C. McClurg & Co., 1912.

[19] *The Eugene City Guard.* "Election Laws and Poll Books." (23 JANUARY 1892): I.

[20] *Evening Capital Journal.* "The Proposed Ballot Law." (22 JANUARY 1891): 3.

[21] *Evening Capital Journal.* "A Victory for the People." (9 FEBRUARY 1891): I.

[22] *Evening Capital Journal.* "The Voice of Labor." (24 JANUARY 1891): 2.

[23] *Evening Capital Journal.* "Republican Platform." (17 APRIL 1890): I.

[24] *The Evening Star.* "William U'Ren, 90, Dies; Oregon Political Reformer."* Washington, D. C., (9 APRIL 1949): A-10.

[25] *The Garfield Banner.* "The Irrepressible Cotter." (22 APRIL 1882): I.

[26] *The Garfield Banner.* *"Valedictory."* and *"Notice."*
      (29 APRIL 1882): 1, 4.

[27] Gaston, Joseph. *The Centennial History of Oregon 1811–1912.*
      VOL. 1 Chicago: The S. J. Clarke Publishing Co., 1912.

[28] Greene, Arthur A. *"A Close View of Lincoln Steffens."*
      The Morning Oregonian (20 MARCH 1907): 10.

[29] von Grueningen, John Paul, Editor. *The Swiss in the United
      States.* Madison, Wisconsin: Swiss-American Historical
      Society, 1940.

[30] Hanks, Patrick, Editor. *Dictionary of American Family Names.*
      Oxford, New York: Oxford University Press, 2003.

[31] Letter from Frank Harper to Jonathan Bourne, Library of
      Congress Manuscript Division.
      www.theodorerooseveltcenter.org, ID=o41400, Theodore
      Roosevelt Digital Library, Dickinson State University.

[32] Hathaway, Milicent L.,. *'Trends in Heights and Weights',
      Yearbook Of Agriculture* 1959. U. S. Department of
      Agriculture, 1959.

[33] Harris & Ewing, photographer. *Jonathan Bourne, Washington
      D.C., 1911.* Photograph. loc.gov/item/2016863692/

[34] *The Hawaiian Gazette.* *"List of Letters Remaining in the General
      Post Office, Honolulu,* SEPT. 30, 1888." (2 OCTOBER 1888): 4.

[35] Hendrick, Burton J. *"The Initiative and Referendum and How
      Oregon Got Them."* McClure's Magazine VOL. 37, NO. 3 (JULY
      1911): 235–248.

[36] Hendrick, Burton J. *"Woodrow Wilson: Political Leader."*
      McClure's Magazine VOL. 38, NO. 1 (NOVEMBER 1911):
      217–231.

[37] Historic American Buildings Survey. *Seth Lewelling House,
      Lot 5, Milwaukie, Clackamas County, Oregon,* 1933.
      Photograph. loc.gov/item/or0130/

[38] Hollingsworth, Charles M.,. *"The So-Called Progressive Movement: Its Real Nature, Causes and Significance."* The *Initiative, Referendum and Recall, The Annals, American Academy of Political and Social Science* VOL. 43 (SEPTEMBER 1912): 32–48.

[39] Hosford, Hester E.,. *Woodrow Wilson: His Career, His Statesmanship, and His Public Policies.* New York and London: G. P. Putnam's Sons, 1912.

[40] Joseph Fels Fund Commission. *Single Tax Conference: Held in New York City* NOVEMBER 19 *and* 20, 1910. Cincinnati: Joseph Fels Fund Commission, 1911.

[41] Kiefer, Daniel. *"What Is the Single Tax?" The Single Tax Review* VOL. 15, NO. 1 (JANUARY–FEBRUARY 1915): 30.

[42] *The Lebanon Express. "Prineville Pickings."* (6 JUNE 1890): 2.

[43] Lockley, Fred. *"Observations and Impressions of the Journal Man." The Oregon Daily Journal* (20 NOVEMBER 1922): 8.

[44] McClintock, Thomas C.,. *"Henderson Luelling, Seth Lewelling and the Birth of the Pacific Coast Fruit Industry." Oregon Historical Quarterly,* VOL. 68, NO. 2 (JUNE 1967): 153–174.

[45] McClintock, Thomas C.,. *"Seth Lewelling, William S. U'Ren and the Birth of the Oregon Progressive Movement." Oregon Historical Quarterly,* VOL. 68, NO. 3 (SEPT. 1967): 196–220.

[46] Mencken, H. L.,. *Prejudices: Third Series.* New York: Alfred A. Knopf (1922).

[47] Miller, Joseph Dana, Editor. *Single Tax Year Book.* New York City: Single Tax Review Publishing Company, 1917.

[48] *The Morning Oregonian. "Finds Africa Shut Up."* (15 OCTOBER 1900): 3.

[49] *The Morning Oregonian. "British Cause Is Just."* (3 JANUARY 1901): 12.

[50] *The Morning Oregonian.* *"Favor New Law."*
(13 JANUARY 1904): 12.

[51] *The Morning Oregonian.* *"People's Power League."*
(15 DECEMBER 1905): 14.

[52] *The Morning Oregonian.* *"Editorial: Now Mr. U'Ren...."*
(17 JULY 1906): 4.

[53] *The Morning Oregonian.* *"Lincoln Steffens Here."*
(14 MARCH 1907): 18.

[54] *The Morning Oregonian.* *"U'Ren Posed as Trance Medium."*
(9 MARCH 1908): 4.

[55] *The Morning Oregonian.* *"Explains Lewelling Deal."*
(10 MARCH 1908): 6.

[56] *The Morning Oregonian.* *"More U'Renism For Oregon?"*
(16 AUGUST 1909): 6.

[57] *The Morning Oregonian.* *"The Ideal and the Real."*
(15 MARCH 1911): 6.

[58] *The Morning Oregonian.* *"Self Control Is Subject of Talk."*
(4 MAY 1911): 1.

[59] *The Morning Oregonian.* *"U'Ren First Gains Gov. Wilson's Ear."*
(18 MAY 1911): 6.

[60] *The Morning Oregonian.* *"Clackamas County scholars...."*
(19 MAY 1911): 10.

[61] *The Morning Oregonian.* *"Leaving It All To U'Ren."*
(20 MAY 1911): 10.

[62] *The Morning Oregonian.* *"A Voice From the U'Renic Tomb."*
(13 FEBRUARY 1913): 10.

[63] *The Morning Oregonian.* *"How To Suppress U'Ren."*
(29 SEPTEMBER 1916): 12.

[64] *Mosier Bulletin.* *"Local."* (1 NOVEMBER 1912): 4.

[65] The National Short Ballot Organization. *The Short Ballot: A Movement to Simplify Politics.* New York: The National Short Ballot Organization, 1915.

[66] Nye, Eric W.,. *Pounds Sterling to Dollars: Historical Conversion of Currency.* From: www.uwyo.edu/numimage/currency.htm

[67] *Ochoco Review.* "Uren & Son Advertisement" (15 OCTOBER 1887): 8.

[68] *Ochoco Review.* "Mark Cary was called home...." (16 AUGUST 1890): 3.

[69] Oregon County Court (Clackamas County); Probate. *"In the Matter of the Estate of T. A. U'Ren, Deceased."* Clackamas, Oregon. (6 APRIL 1901).

[70] *Oregon City Courier.* "Lincoln Steffens Talks on Graft." (22 MARCH 1907): 4.

[71] *Oregon City Courier.* "W. S. U'Ren, comes out for United States Senator."* (28 FEBRUARY 1908): 1.

[72] *Oregon City Courier-Herald.* "Professional Men." (3 JANUARY 1902): 39.

[73] *Oregon City Courier-Herald.* "Uren and Schuebel Advertisement."* (30 AUGUST 1901).

[74] *Oregon City Enterprise.* "A Lively Meeting." (21 JANUARY 1898): 1.

[75] *Oregon City Enterprise.* "Lincoln Steffens Visits This City." (15 MARCH 1907): 1.

[76] *Oregon City Enterprise.* "Garden Spot in Oregon City." (13 AUGUST 1909): 3.

[77] *Oregon City Enterprise.* "W. S. U'Ren..." (20 AUGUST 1909): 1.

[78] *Oregon City Enterprise.* "Trifle Gossipy." (7 JULY 1911): 3.

[79] *The Oregon Daily Journal.* "Lincoln Steffens on His Way to the Coast." (3 JANUARY 1907): 7.

[80] *The Oregon Daily Journal.* "W. S. U'Ren Proud of His Association With Joseph Fels." (23 FEBRUARY 1914): 7.

[81] *The Oregon Mist.* "The New Ballot Law." (19 FEBRUARY 1892): 2.

[82] Pach Brothers. "*Woodrow Wilson, head-and-shoulders portrait, facing left.*" Photograph. C. 1912. loc.gov/item/96522632/

[83] Parker, Mabel Frances Childs. *The U'Rens: Cornwall to Gladstone 1834 to 1926.* Booklet.

[84] Pease, Lute. "*The Initiative and Referendum—Oregon's 'Big Stick'.*" The Pacific Monthly. VOL. 17 (1907): 563–575.

[85] Peterman, Alexander L.,. *Elements of Civil Government.* New York, Cincinnati, Chicago: American Book Company, 1916. www.gutenberg.org/files/15018/15018-h/15018-h.htm

[86] Piott, Steven L.,. *Giving Voters a Voice: The Origin of the Initiative and Referendum in America.* Columbia and London: University of Missouri Press, 2003.

[87] Poet, S. E.,. "*The Story of Tin Cup, Colorado.*" The Colorado Magazine. VOL. 9, NO. 1 (JANUARY 1932): 30–38.

[88] Puter, S. A. D.,. *Looters of the Public Domain.* Portland, Oregon: The Portland Printing House, 1908.

[89] R. L. Polk & Co. *Portland City Directory* 1891. Portland, Oregon (1891): 626.

[90] Rash, Janessa. "*The Family History of Janessa Rash.*" (2017). Your Family in History: Hist 550/700.50, 2017: https://digitalcommons.pittstate.edu/hist550/50/

[91] *Rocky Mountain Sun.* "Personal." (7 OCTOBER 1882): 2.

[92] *Rocky Mountain Sun.* "Mining Notes." (7 AUGUST 1886): 2.

[93] *Rocky Mountain Sun. "City Items."* (25 JUNE 1887): 2.

[94] Letter from Theodore Roosevelt to William Simon U'Ren,
Library of Congress Manuscript Division.
https://www.theodorerooseveltcenter.org, ID=o217103,
Theodore Roosevelt Digital Library, Dickinson State
University.

[95] Roosevelt, Theodore. *"The People of the Pacific Coast."*
The Outlook. (2 SEPTEMBER 1911): 159–162.

[96] *San Francisco Call. "Personal Mentions."* (11 APRIL 1907)

[97] Snyder, Keith. *Prineville Business History:* 1868–1922.
Crook County Historical Society, 2004.

[98] South Africa; U'Ren, Thomas Andrew. Probate,
Johannesburg, Gauteng, South Africa, Pietermaritzburg
Archives (formerly Natal State Archives), South Africa; FHL
microfilm 1,367,260 (1902).

14 FEBRUARY 2019. "South Africa, Transvaal, Probate Records
from the Master of the Supreme Court, 1869–1958,"
database with images, FamilySearch.
https://familysearch.org/ark:/61903/1:1:QLQ7-5VKJ

[99] *State Rights Democrat. "Democratic Platform."* (2 MAY 1890): 1.

[100] Steffens, Lincoln. *The Autobiography of Lincoln Steffens.* New
York: Harcourt, Brace and Company, 1931.

[101] Steffens, Lincoln. *"The Taming of the West: Discovery of the
Land Fraud System; A Detective Story." The American
Magazine.* VOL. 64 (SEPTEMBER 1907): 489–505.

[102] Steffens, Lincoln. *"The Taming of the West: Heney Grapples the
Oregon Land Graft." The American Magazine.* VOL. 64
(OCTOBER 1907): 585–602.

[103] Steffens, Lincoln. *"U'Ren—The Law-Giver." The American
Magazine.* VOL. 65 (MARCH 1908): 527–40.

[104] Steffens, Lincoln. *Upbuilders*. New York: Doubleday, Page & Company, 1909.

[105] Sullivan, J. W.,. *Direct Legislation by the Citizenship Through the Initiative and Referendum*. New York: True Nationalist Publishing, 1892.

[106] *The Sunday Oregonian*. *"Hatless U'Ren And Paget Deny Portland Is Rainy."* (18 NOVEMBER 1917): 18.

[107] *The Sunday Oregonian*. *"Leaves for Johannesburg."* (22 JULY 1900): 20.

[108] *The Sunday Oregonian*. *"Going to Settle His Brother's Estate."* (29 JULY 1900): 7.

[109] *The Sunday Oregonian*. *"The Late E. W. Bingham."* (10 JANUARY 1904): 21.

[110] *The Tin Cup Banner*. *"A Fat Legacy."* (3 JUNE 1882): 4.

[111] *The Tin Cup Record*. *"City Marshall Harry Rivers Shot and Killed."* (11 MARCH 1882): 1.

[112] *The Tin Cup Record*. *"The Pen Is Mightier Than the Sword."* (22 APRIL 1882): 1.

[113] U'Ren, W. S.,. 1900; Passport Application, source certificate #30886, Passport Applications, 1795–1905., Roll 561, NARA microfilm publications M1490 and M1372 (Washington D.C.: National Archives and Records Administration, n.d.).

16 MARCH 2018, United States Passport Applications, 1795–1925, database with images, FamilySearch. https://familysearch.org/ark:/61903/1:1:QVJP-75X7

[114] U'Ren, W. S.,. *"How Oregon Secured Pure Elections."* *La Follette's Weekly Magazine*. (3 APRIL 1909): 7.

[115] U'Ren, W. S.,. *"Results of the Initiative and Referendum in Oregon."* *Proceedings of the American Political Science Association*. VOL. 4 Fourth Annual Meeting (1907): 193–197.

[116] U'Ren, W. S.,. *"Six Years of the Initiative and Referendum in Oregon."* The City Club Bulletin, City Club of Chicago VOL. 2, NO. 38 (26 MAY 1909): 465–478.

[117] Unknown. *The election.,* 1857. Photograph. loc.gov/item/97512421/

[118] Unknown. *The election–At the polls / W.J.H.,* 1857. Photograph. loc.gov/item/97512416/

[119] Unknown. *John Hipple Mitchell, of Oregon, between* 1870 *and* 1880. Photograph. loc.gov/item/2017893156/

[120] Unknown. *Roosevelt at Eugene, Or.,* APRIL 5. Photograph. 1911. loc.gov/item/2013649557/

[121] Unknown. *Theodore Roosevelt, half-length portrait, facing front.* Photograph. C. 1911. loc.gov/item/2013649808/

[122] Unknown. *George Henry Williams, of Oregon, between* 1865 *and* 1880. Photograph. loc.gov/item/2017895123/

[123] Western Historical Publishing Company. *An Illustrated History of Central Oregon: Embracing Wasco, Sherman, Gilliam, Wheeler, Crook, Lake, and Klamath Counties, State of Oregon.* Spokane, Washington: Western Historical Publishing Company, 1905.

[124] Willis, William L.,. *History of Sacramento County, California.* Los Angeles, California: Historic Record Company, 1913.

[125] Wilson, Woodrow. *The New Freedom: A Call for the Emancipation of the Generous Energies of a People.* New York and Garden City: Doubleday, Page & Company, 1913.

[126] Wortman, Roy T.,. *"Denver's Anti-Chinese Riot, 1880."* The Colorado Magazine. VOL. 42, NO. 4 (Fall 1965): 275–291.

INDEX

ACKNOWLEDGMENTS

THE EDITORS ARE GRATEFUL FOR THE ASSISTANCE OF

Janice Bahns • Michael Collins

Craig T. Danielson • Juanita Williams

REFERENCE ASSISTANCE

Crook County Historical Center—A.R. Bowman Museum

Maggie Pando—The Dalles Wasco Co. Library

Deschutes Public Library

EDITORIAL RESOURCES

The Chicago Manual of Style • *Garner's Modern English Usage*

WORLD WIDE WEB RESOURCES

archive.org • books.google.com

coloradohistoricnewspapers.org • oregonnews.uoregon.edu

TOOLS USED TO MAKE THIS BOOK

Macintosh iMac Desktop Computer from Apple Inc.

LaTeX Document Preparation System

Sublime Text • TeX Live Utility • TexShop

TECHNICAL RESOURCES

latex-project.org • tug.org/mactex • tex.stackexchange.com